Paul Valéry

Titles by William Kluback on Valéry

Paul Valéry: Philosophical Reflections (1987)

Paul Valéry: The Search for Intelligence (1993)

Paul Valéry: Illusions of Civilization (1996)

Paul Valéry: The Continuous Search for Reality (1997)

Paul Valéry: The Realms of the Analecta (1998)

PETER LANG
New York • Washington, D.C./Baltimore • Boston
Bern • Frankfurt am Main • Berlin • Vienna • Paris

William Kluback

Paul Valéry

The Statesman of the Intellect

PETER LANG
New York • Washington, D.C./Baltimore • Boston
Bern • Frankfurt am Main • Berlin • Vienna • Paris

Library of Congress Cataloging-in-Publication Data

Kluback, William.
Paul Valéry: the statesman of the intellect / William Kluback.
p. cm.
Includes bibliographical references.
1. Valéry, Paul, 1871–1945—Political and social views. 2. Valéry, Paul,
1871–1945—Philosophy. 3. Descartes, René, 1596–1650—Influence. I. Title.
PQ2643.A26Z65674   841'.912—dc21   98-42379
ISBN 0-8204-4113-9

Die Deutsche Bibliothek-CIP-Einheitsaufnahme

Kluback, William:
Paul Valéry: the statesman of the intellect / William Kluback.
–New York; Washington, D.C./Baltimore; Boston; Bern;
Frankfurt am Main; Berlin; Vienna; Paris: Lang.
ISBN 0-8204-4113-9

Cover design by Andy Ruggirello

The paper in this book meets the guidelines for permanence and durability
of the Committee on Production Guidelines for Book Longevity
of the Council of Library Resources.

© 1999 Peter Lang Publishing, Inc., New York

Printed in the United States of America

Dedicated to those physicians of the soul
who bring healing and care

Table of Contents

Preface

This is the sixth volume of my Valéry studies. The volume is dedicated to both Valéry's interpretation of his role as a political thinker and to the effect of Descartes upon his view of Self. The conclusion is simple. I maintain that no political thought is possible without the experience of the *Cogito*. There is a mixture between autobiography and theoretical thinking, between subjectivity and objectivity, assuming that these two terms are nothing more than masks of the same substance. These are the masks which we confront, having decided upon an attitude that suits a political point of view. After realizing how deeply skepticism is a part of our thinking, how deeply we are dependent upon consciousness, we find that a political point of view is deeply involved in the *Cogito*. In that experience lies the consciousness of thinking. Thinking is a political act. For the sake of simplicity, we say that man is a highly complex and undefinable being who is totally dependent upon the undetermined nature of time, and the experience of limited space.

Paul Valéry has impressed us with his utter devotion to Descartes, not as a scholar of each of his particular works, but to his autobiographical texts. These are fundamentally significant for us. They reveal the close and intimate relationship between thinking and the personality of the thinker. The *Who* is as vital to us as the *What*. Who a man is, is inseparable from what a man does. This Valéry made very clear. It characterized the nature of his political work at the League of Nations. We have little difficulty in recognizing the stature which Valéry achieved on the world scene. He was *the* European intellectual whose voice flowed beyond borders, whose name elicited respect and power. Valéry was a powerful man in a prudent and courageous way.

It was not until I finished this last volume that I realized how deeply influential Valéry was. He was far more than a French poet and essayist, he was the intellectual statesman of the free world, commanding those who chose to think and take seriously the world about them. Even more significant was the fact that his language brought to the mind of every thinker a universal message of freedom and responsibility, a message Valéry himself embodied. He once wrote that if a man yearned to accomplish something, he would have to sacrifice all other values and interests. This single-minded dedication to the universal struggle for freedom marked the greatness of Valéry's personality.

If we think back to Europe before 1945, perhaps before 1939, we realize how significant the voice of Valéry was. We hear it today. It has gone through time, talking to those who are still concerned with the problem of freedom, but under new circumstances. We may spend years writing our imaginary discussions with Valéry. We will never exhaust the greatness of the man. He comes back to us again and again, wanting to be heard, knowing that his words are yet to be understood. How foolish are those who believe that they have fully understood him! They make but a few inroads. They take the few for the many. Valéry is the symbol of the never-ending search for the *Cogito*. He, together with Descartes, has shown us a way. It is so very difficult to follow, but follow we must. What choice do we really have?

Introduction

We are in a medieval alchemist's chamber. We are reading from Goethe's *Faust* II, Act II. The heading is called "Laboratory." We will explain this in a moment. I would like to mention that Valéry had spoken of Goethe at the Sorbonne on April 30, 1932, commemorating the 100th anniversary of Goethe's death. Valéry's evaluation of Goethe seems to be the one that would be suitable to him. He saw some similarities between himself and Goethe. Valéry remarked: "In the evening of his days in the heart of Europe, himself the center of attraction and the admiration of all intelligent people, the center of the greatest curiosity, the subtlest and noblest Master of the Art of Living and of deepening the taste for living, Genial Lover of All things, *Pontifex Maximus,* which is to say, the great builder of bridges between the centuries and the forms of culture, Goethe grew to a luminous old age among his antiques, his herbals, his engravings, his books, his thoughts, his confidants. As the hours grew late, the least word he spoke became an oracle" ("Address in Honor of Goethe, in *Masters and Friends,* 174).

I can't imagine the last six years of Valéry's life without the madness which afflicted it. He envisioned a crumbling civilization. It played havoc with his serene belief in the *Cogito,* in the wonders that emerged from the works of Mallarmé, Montesquieu, Leonardo da Vinci, Einstein. The tradition he adored had died. Never again would Western civilization believe so deeply in its intellectual tradition with that remarkable confidence which Valéry embodied and felt. Totalitarianism and many of its forms had destroyed his faith, his visions, his hopes. The more we encounter Valéry, the more we realize how far we are from the tradition he admired and represented. Absurdity had become a subtle word for that.

We have come a long way from our beliefs in knowledge, beauty, and goodness as the masks of man. We have left ourselves in a cynical world that is ruled by an unbearable skepticism. We are orphaned from the reason. The latter has slipped away, and we doubt if it ever existed, but it did. We have become exiles. We listen daringly to Valéry's remark concerning Descartes: "I think, therefore I am." "This is not a piece of reasoning," he said, "it's a fist coming down on a table to corroborate words in the mind" (1910). Let's listen to a few epigrammatic comments from the *Notebooks* about Pascal:

> Pascal is more exciting to the mind than Descartes; Descartes excites the will. (1926)
> I like Descartes because of the great, simple purity of the man, the solidarity of his thought, the general air of honesty and an order apparent in his whole manner. (1924)
> Descartes sees the *power* of thought, Pascal its impotence. (1924)
> You must confess, Monsieur des Cartes, that to say "I am" is to say absolutely nothing; and to say "I think" is to say: "I talk to myself, I see, or operate in a certain way – I compare."

I have considered Descartes as the fundamental figure in Valéry's approach to reality. He admired many figures, but Descartes was its greatest expression. Descartes's *Cogito* brought the world into existence. It spoke to us not only of the Art of Living, but of the Art of Thinking, the precious, and most dangerous of arts man has ever practiced. Man is a thinker at a frightening expense to the Self.

I end these scattered opinions with the description of a scene I mentioned in the first paragraph of this introduction. I do this because I realize that we are at the beginning of a new era of civilization: the human creation of man and animal.

We listen for a moment to Goethe's *Faust*. Wagner speaks:

> The shadows have begun to be less dark,
> and in the inmost vial
> something is glowing like a living ember
> and, like a glorious carbuncle,
> initiates the darkness with red lightning flashes.
> A clear, white light can now be seen!
> If only, this time, I don't lose it!
> O Lord! what is that clatter at the door?

Wagner speaks again to Mephistopheles. He says:

> Old-fashioned procreation
> is something we reject as folly.
> The feeble force that was life's starting point,
> like the compelling strength that from it sprang
> and took and gave, ordained to shape its own design
> assimilating first like elements, and then unlike

* *

but human beings, with their splendid talents
must henceforth have a higher, nobler order.

(*Faust* II, act 2, Laboratory
[Princeton: Princeton University
Press, 1994], 175-76)

Valéry looked into the lands of a new order. His vision was not clear. He saw it under an unyielding and suffocating mist. There were only premonitions. A frightening veil hung over a melancholic despair. There was a limp heaviness. We bent with it. He could not give voice to it. It overflowed his breathing. He extended his hand to Voltaire and felt comfort in the old believer, in the man whose sensitivities were very highly developed, and who took seriously the humane survival of humankind. Valéry stood close to him, feeling the pending doom which slowly advanced toward Western European civilization. He saw no promised land. He didn't even hear the exciting but demoniacal words of Wagner:

> It's rising, flashing, piling up –
> another moment and it's done!
> A grand design may seem insane at first;
> but in the future chance will seem absurd,
> and such a brain as this, intended for great
> thoughts, will in its turn create a thinker too
> (Laboratory, 176).

We read these lines. We are haunted by them. We realize that man can create himself, not only theoretically but actually. The Homunculus frees itself from Wagner's vial. It is free, created by a master. The opening lines of the divine exit have been sounded. Technology is all about us. Wagner has drawn a secret from it. His work is marked out for him. He will do it well. Nations of created men and women will produce armies of cloned children. They will fight their wars totally controlled and dominated by their inventors. These will be the chosen ones. These will be the damned ones. All sorts of possibilities will invade our unlimited minds.

Our ideas will become reality. *The vial is broken.* A new epoch has begun. Descartes has been left behind. The *Cogito* fades away. The God that brought it into existence is no more. There was a madness in the *Cogito,* a productive and fascinating human belief in God. The *I* has lost its bearings. Its truth can no longer be recognized. The god Janus makes everything seem inadequate, and yet possible. He is the cruelest among the gods. He shows the whirlwind. We lose ourselves in it.

Valéry watches Descartes pass away. The new world is spoken for by Mephistopheles, who now turns to his audience and says wearily: "The fact is, we remain dependent on the creatures we ourselves have made"

(Laboratory, 179). The new powers belong to these new creatures. We can never fix or direct the movement from creator to created. We watch, we conjecture, we wonder. I still use the words of Descartes. They belong to a Voltaire, or to a Valéry. Wagner has put them aside. The Homunculus tells Wagner:

> Why, you'll stay home and do what's most important.
> Peruse your ancient manuscripts,
> collect life's elements as they direct;
> then put the parts together – cautiously –
> and think about the What and, even more, the How! –
> Meanwhile I shall explore the world a bit
> and so perhaps discover to dot the i's.
> (Laboratory, 179).

The reader can now proceed to my text. There I hope I have brought him closer to the genius of Valéry, the last European. In this genius lies one of the finest expressions of the European mind. Its era may be over. I have no idea of what is coming. Goethe has given us some hints, although he didn't intend to do so. We read Goethe differently today. We read into him. We hear Mephistopheles differently, much more seriously. We wonder if the nobility of the *Cogito* will ever fade away, but has it not already faded away? Will we ever lose consciousness? We are frightened by the possibility, and we are quiet. There is nothing further that we can do. We are being created by others. Is there a message that can be heard? We can sit silently and read John of Patmos and wonder if his work offers us something. We don't know. We hope that we know what we are doing. Too often we have been told that we know not what we do.

We leave the book to the reader, the one who will follow both his knowledge and his imagination. He has heard Kant's remark *aude sapere*, dare to know. I would add: dare to imagine, dare to feel. I doubt that the philosopher of Königsberg would object. He was a tolerant man. He did create a revolution and handled it well. Valéry would have appreciated him if he had known him well. Kant was a nobly honest man. This motto "dare to know" is a pleasant saying that leads us everywhere and nowhere. We are slowly shifting away from a world created in the image of the *I think* to one that awakens us to the fact that much of our thinking has already occurred. We think only because what we encounter has already been thought. This leaves us in an unknown position, always attempting to discover the nature of thought, knowing that nature is already known. It, as yet, doesn't belong to our awareness.

We leave our subject with the odd feeling that we have gone from paradox to paradox, from parable to parable. With the paradox under one arm and the parable under the other, we walk into eternal exile. As we walk , we realize that no thought is possible without a recognition of events. From the very beginnings of our discussion, we listed the events that were pertinent to it. We can't merely speak of subject and object, thought and experience. They exist together. Reality is their coexistence, their co-relationship. Things occur whether I think of them or not. The problem lies in the awareness of them, but awareness changes nothing. It does make change possible. Forget events! Thought is sterile. Forget thinking, and events are chaotic. They are nothing more than the scattered bits offered to the god Janus.

This is the last of my six volumes of Valéry studies. I have new paths to follow, but never will Valéry be distant from me. He is a spiritual companion. For the past twenty years, I have tried to approach him through his published works and his *Notebooks,* or *Cahiers.* I discovered that reading was only the beginning of the process of comprehension. Reading induces further reading, but above all, it entices us to reread. It is in this rereading – however far away it may be from the first reading – that we find the essential moment of thinking. Here the opening finds possibilities of expression. Here the cycle begins its journey of renewal and expansion. Here circularity changes opinions into thoughts, openings into repetitions, changing slightly, but powerfully what was the before and what becomes the after. We are in the midst of thinking. I reveal to you what it means to be in the midst of thinking, to feel the powers of *Cartesius Redivivus.*

1

Paul Valéry: From Poet to Statesman

The more I seek to avoid speaking of the theory-practice dichotomy the more I fall into its enticement, and I speak of it. What is it that I want to speak of when I confront the problem of civilization? No such problem exists. I confront an illusion. Man is what he is: a being who thinks when he wants to think, an acting being of feelings, of metaphors and imagery when he uses his imagination. It is the same man or woman who does both. Yet sameness does not indicate that within the person there are conflicting attitudes and characteristics which are incommensurate with each other. Man is a contentious being. He struggles with the community about him and with the attitudes within him. I wonder if thinking is radically separable from feeling, if pleasure doesn't accompany touch as well as it accompanies thought. When we approach man, we encounter a personality for whom thinking is only one expression. We are startled by the fact that some people are greater as personalities than they are thinkers, while some are greater as thinkers than they are as personalities. This causes us a great deal of confusion and we return to the dualism we want to avoid. How magnificent it would be if we could equate man the doer with man the thinker, knowing that man is both, inseparably both! Why do the parts run from each other, become opponents, and struggle with each other for domination? We prefer to describe dichotomies than seek explanations for them. We look at man in despair. We want to escape a being in whom feeling and thinking run away from each other, pursuing different ends and ultimately wanting to control each other. I cite a few lines of a poem of John Wilmot, Earl of Rochester. The poem is called "A Satyr against Mankind." I chose these lines:

> But man with smiles, embraces, friendship, praise,
> Most humanly his fellow's life betrays,

7

With voluntary pains works his distress,
Not through necessity but wantonness.

> (John Wilmot, Earl of Rochester,
> *The Complete Works*, Penguin,
> 1994, 73)

This wise poet described man well. He was not plagued by theoretical problems. He wrote from body and soul which in him was a whole, the whole who was called John Wilmot (1647-80), friend of King Charles II, satirist and poet, a lover of the jolly life, but it is not the satirist who is of interest to us, but the statesman, the gentleman.

I believe that Paul Valéry surpassed his work as poet, literary critic, and human observer to become the statesman of Europe, a philosopher-king in the Platonic sense. He embodied in his stature the quality of thinker who surpassed his specialty, and his academic recognition. He became a world figure, a man whose word was heard everywhere by every serious man and woman. This recognition didn't come as a satisfaction for the scholar of his particular field. He was indeed thanked for his literary clarification, for his valuable insights which can be quoted and which helped supply the heap of footnotes men and women need to protect their status. Paul Valéry gave the scholars more than they needed. What he gave humankind was a rare gift. He gave it his concern for human freedom. He appeared on the stage of political life, and to this stage he called the thinkers and philosophers. He asked them to assume the role of politically responsible men. The dangers of Nazism, Fascism, and Communism clearly threatened the survival of European civilization and as the thirties advanced, the dangers became more and more explicit. Valéry needed to speak.

Aristotle remarked in the *Nicomachean Ethics* that politics is a science of experience whose end is not knowledge but action. This is an extremely sharp separation. Knowledge is not completely divorced from action, but, in fact, makes action intelligible and meaningful. There is the action of the mob and the action of the statesman, there is the concern for ethics or the willingness to set it aside. It is either significant or insignificant. In his introduction to the English translations of Valéry, entitled *History and Politics*, the Spanish statesman Salvador de Madariaga wrote: "For some reason or other, ever since Machiavelli was praised by Bacon for showing what human relations are instead of pointing to what they should be, a certain type of scientific or positivist student of man has endeavored to eliminate ethics from the world of men in society – as if the need most human beings feel for decency in behavior were not a part of the picture in its own right as much as the rest. There is no denying the fact that Valéry is prone to take that point of view in his political writings" (introduction to *History and Politics,* Pantheon Books, 1962, xxxiv).

This entrance into the political world was one of the deepest challenges encountered by Valéry. It challenged his ability to organize the free world against the threat of totalitarianism. It is a rejection of a theoretical world of ideas and ideals which led nowhere. It enjoyed only listening to itself in grandiose tones appealing more to the heavens than to the world. No word nor thought could remove his fear that European civilization was crumbling. History, Valéry was convinced, could neither tell a believable story nor convince us that it could not be told differently. All we needed was a more or less imaginative historian. Valéry often spoke of the crisis of the mind. We wonder why this theme doesn't return often to our discussion. We have become students of descriptions. Few of us wonder how we have been affected by what we have seen and contemplated. François Valéry, Valéry's son, noted in the preface which preceded the introduction of Salvador de Madariaga that Valéry's political thought was "a by-product of his intense intellectual activity, turned more inward than outward" (preface to *History and Politics,* xvi).

It may be alleged that Valéry was not, in the strictest sense, a political thinker. We know that thinking and doing have political consequences. The creation of a society whose ideals and attitudes are guided by freedom must make the conscious effort of fostering leaders, statesmen, who believe in freedom. Where this concern is dominant, political thinking is inseparable from action. Society develops a commitment to the rights of men and women avoiding the necessity of state interference. This is an illusion. Politics remains the work of the statesmen, of the men whose efforts are to increase the number of thinking citizens, of those who are aware that freedom doesn't belong to an elite but to the education of the public. Valéry sought what François Valéry called intellectual capital. It is this increasing capital which would make it possible for a democratic public to come into being, a public who actively participates in political debate, who thinks with and against the ideas they confront, who understands courage and the need for action, but even more understands the price which leaders have to pay for these virtues.

Salvador de Madariaga told us that he came to know Valéry when he joined the Committee on Arts and Letters of the Institute of Intellectual Cooperation of the League of Nations. De Madariaga noted that the aim of the committee was to establish a society of human beings whose concern was principally communication among themselves, communication through letters. In fact, de Madariaga wrote to Valéry. We will speak later of the letter and Valéry's response. Referring to Valéry's answer, de Madariaga remarked: "It is, nevertheless, a superb statement of the theme of understanding between men and nations – that theme which will still embody our prime need and our prime hope, precisely because the society of the minds which we advocated is still rent asunder by an abyss. But this abyss, does it cut across thought or across the faith of men?" (introduction, xxxvi).

Politics belongs not to the present but to the future, not to our descriptions of life but to the hopes we put into them. Human courage is a virtue, the middle way between cowardice and foolhardiness; a way which urges us to fight for life, knowing it can't survive without the battle. No philosopher made us more aware of this courage than did William James. He knew that there had to be "a will to believe" if a society were to survive. This will can't be created by the intellect. Intellectuals have so often betrayed us that we rush from feeling their betrayal. They have labeled men and women of fear and compromise. Lost is James's spirit of courageous confrontation which he expressed magnificently in a talk in 1895 at Harvard. We cite the famous last paragraph of the essay "Is Life Worth Living?": "Be not afraid of life. Believe that life *is* worth living and your belief will help create the fact. The 'scientific proof' that you are right may not be clear before the day of judgment is reached. But the faithful fighters of this hour, or the beings that then and there will represent them, may then turn to the fainthearted, who here decline to go on, with words like those with which Henry IV greeted the tardy Crillon after a great victory had been gained: Hang yourself, brave Crillon! We fought at Araques and you were not there." ("Is Life Worth Living?" in *The Will to Believe* [Cambridge: Harvard University Press, 1979], 56). (The incident referred to Voltaire's *La Henriade,* to a letter from Henry IV of France to Louis Berton de Crillon supposedly written after the battle of Arques in 1589.)

We have supposedly made a long leap from pragmatic belief to political audacity, that Valéry in his own way, toward the end of his life, not only accepted but chose. He rejected the man of contemplation and became a man of action. This division was clearly enunciated for us by Aristotle. He listed for us three manners of living. We could be seekers of pleasure, of action, or of contemplation. Valéry chose action. He disdained the vagueness of the contemplative life and the abstract idea. He refused it adamantly in his personal life. The European crisis plagued him. There was never a period in his life when he didn't carefully follow in some way or another the course of political events. He served for twenty-two years as a private secretary to Edouard Lebey, the director of the Havas News Agency. There was no separation from politics.

We are concerned deeply with this idea of the European mind. It is not an abstraction. It is meaningful because it is a factual and existential reality, a concrete experience, a force which conditions and forms life. It is an inescapable condition. If it embodies the values we live by, those which form our education and our ideals, we must then ask if this is a civilization which is also worth fighting for. These may be values which we find uncompromisable. They have a right to remain untarnished and uncompromised.

In 1935, Valéry, in an interview published in *Les Nouvelles littéraires* spoke of "L'Esprit européan." It was a short but striking interview. Valéry remarked that the European spirit "may be considered first of all as a sort of myth in our own minds – a desire for *understanding and exchange* which we cannot imagine our minds doing without. For example, the idea of *Shakespeare* is an integral part of French or Italian or German culture" ("The European Spirit," in *History and Politics,* 326). If we understand the European mind as a myth, we are willing to conceive it as an act of faith, a way we must follow even if it leads to disaster. Our faith in Europe conditions and forms our existence. We are its children. The politics which emerge from it bring with it inevitable consequences. Myths which are the imaginary poetry of civilization bring us into their embrace. We are participants in a myth remembered from a past we can't set aside. Refuse to read the classics of a civilization, and you have freed yourself of its myths. Free yourself of the myths, and you are free to destroy or radically alter civilization. The civilization no longer commands your loyalty. It has become a series of chaotic remembrances, fragments of values and arbitrary forms. These are there to be denied, manipulated, or reordered. Living exclusively in the self is the indifferent architect who has lost his care for the material which floats about him.

The notion of the European mind has become a belief, but we wonder if such a belief can withstand the shock not only of two world wars, but of the banal moral terror we became aware of in Germany's concentration camps and the slave camps of the Soviet Union. We can't shunt the problem aside by isolating the terrors in personal historical accounts in the cinema, in museums, in statistics. The terror lies in events which belong to the work of ordinary people who acted under orders and did their jobs without thought. If ordered, men and women did what was necessary to protect their positions.

People don't have moral problems. They do good and bad things indifferently. Their survival matters. They never like or dislike their fellow human beings. There was no moral crisis. This is a term invented by intellectuals. Arguments and discussions need classification and concepts. We discovered that men kill each other easily and indifferently. The twentieth century revealed how easily this is accomplished with engineering and the orderly use of transportation and communication.

Valéry made a remark which caused us no consternation. He said: "I have no faith in *direct* political action by *men of intellect*" ("The European

Spirit," 327). The men of intellect have usually dealt easily with the powers that be. They enjoyed their presence. We need only read of the vast numbers of German intellectuals who eagerly served the Nazi state, the crowds of collaborators who emerged from the French body politic. We read, with moral and aesthetic shock, about the society that developed around Ernst Jünger in Paris. There is no connection between aesthetic contemplation and pleasure, and moral feeling and responsibility.

We listen further to Valéry A sentence is never adequate. He continues in a sad and painful way. Referring to the men of intellect, he said: "They thereby lose their own virtues without acquiring the powers of professional politicians. Politics, political action, and political forms, are necessarily inferior values and inferior activities of the mind, for politics can exist only by working upon the automatisms, the myths, all the demons of the mind which, on the contrary, we ought to try rather to dominate and exorcise. I find in politics an irresponsible, complex, and contradictory interpretation of history, which is one of the most powerful instruments of political illusion" ("The European Spirit," 327–28). We find it difficult to comprehend these remarks. The political state is a natural end of human associations proceeding from household, to community, to the state. In fact, as we read Valéry's remarks, we step away from them shocked and distraught, feeling that what must be a noble concern, a responsible activity, has been set aside as inferior. We hand over to inferior men the purpose and good of the state, turning our backs and seeking higher and superior activities.

Even more startling is Valéry's belief that "in the field of political discussion and political action, I find all the elements that I reject, that anyone rejects, at these moments when each of us is at last *himself* – that is, able to devote himself to the pure, direct action of his mind" ("The European Spirit," 328). I find myself astounded by Valéry's remarks. This glorification of the self retreating from political society forces us to feel that those who believe that political responsibility is the highest achievement of the rational and reasonable man have been degraded and scorned, that the contemplative life has been ruled higher, and thus more worthy than political life. Is this not a falsehood?

If we continue reading the interview, and we must if we are anxious about Valéry's remarks, we come to the words: "I believe that perfectly free thought, entirely disengaged from any desire for power and any intention of making propaganda as detached and disciplined as possible, can *still* play a part" ("The European Spirit," 328). If this means that the intellectual must avoid political activity in order to prevent self-corruption, then we become even more despairing. The role of intellectuals becomes priestly. We saw their compromising and dishonest role in the student uprisings in 1969. We need only turn to the sad and disturbing case of Harvard University. Academic courage is a rare and nonexportable item and finds little satisfaction in the mind which is trained in contemplation and self-consciousness. I read these words and I think of Lord Acton's belief in the corrupting consequences of power. If this is Valéry's fear, it is legitimate but demeaning. The work of the intellectual can't be protected. We must assume that he has the moral capacity to protect the integrity of his work, the values which have created him, and to which he is obviously loyal.

The intellectual is a creature of his values. These embody a culture of sophistry, a belief in the notion that he is the measure of the truth and falsity of all that is or is not. We are born students of Protagoras. He taught us deconstruction, i.e., he taught us how to justify our egoism to the degree that the idea of the *Politikos* has faded away and with it has gone the inseparability of political responsibility and moral development. The moral is nothing more than what is suitable for the moment.

At the end of his statement, Valéry spoke of the European tradition as a collective awareness of values, of technological power. He then acknowledged the awareness of "civil and spiritual freedom." These are values which inspire "all who set a high price on those results." The question which emerges from this acknowledgment is: How can they be protected if they are not fought for, if there is no willingness to be political in the finest sense of the word: the assumption of political responsibility?

This interview leaves us baffled. We are shaken by the absence of the moral dimension, by its lack of persuasiveness and ideality. We find it difficult to speak of the devotion "to pure, direct action of the mind." We don't easily escape Aristotle or the rhetorical belief that politics is an art of action demanding the powers of persuasion and conviction which the philosopher Chaim Perelman spoke about so eloquently. He reestablished the art of rhetoric as the source of genuine humanism. It seems to me that in ignoring this art, Valéry could not approach a valid theory of politics. The latter doesn't exist without rhetoric, without an understanding of the great rhetoricians of Athens and speeches of Cicero. Men are political not through the theoretical sciences based upon a logic of clear and distinct ideas, but through a logic of assumptions and possibilities, the logic of a Demosthenes, a Protagoras, or a Cicero. Valéry passed by the art of rhetoric developed in Renaissance Italy to immerse himself in Cartesian logic and Leonardo's experimentations. The consequences were radical. They deeply affected Valéry's notion of truth.

We assume the rhetorical view that every aspect of human creativity has a political consequence, that it can be translated into a political attitude. Human creativity, whether it be in the arts or the sciences, necessitates a consciousness of freedom, or the responsibility for its neglect. It necessitates the ability to be persuasive, to show the absolute need for freedom and the meaning of political responsibility. We must be convinced of these ideas. I return to Salvador de Madariaga's comment that Valéry seems to have fallen into that group of thinkers who are more given to describe what is, rather than to stress what should be. In this case, a little more of William James would have been of great help. We hesitate to classify Valéry too quickly. Our story has just begun. There are many other things we have to evaluate.

In 1922, Valéry gave a lecture at the University of Zurich called "The European." We need to know how he conceived of Europe. What was its mythic and nonmythic quality, what were the beliefs it embodied and the consequence of these beliefs? This is a question which has often plagued us, making us feel that the more histories we write, the more we are preparing for the death of this civilization. History books have always made me feel as if we are exhausting the remembrances of a civilization that is passing away. If it is passing away, I wonder if there are still values to be defended. There are epitaphs to be written.

At the beginning of his lecture, Valéry observed that four years after a world war which had taken from society a majority of its creative young people, "we are still uneasy...anxious...as though [the storm] was just now going to break.... We ponder on what is gone, we are almost ruined by what has been ruined; we do not know what is to come, and have some reason to fear it" ("The European," in *History and Politics*, 307). He continued his remarks with a statement that resounded unabated in the years to come: "*Nous sommes une génération très infortunée*" (*Pléiade*, note, 1:1000). If this were so in 1922, it was so in 1935, in 1945, and is so in 1997. Politics deals with an unfortunate world. It deals with human gloom and none of us can escape *cette impression de ténèbres*. Valéry knew well how to test the pulse of the civilization in which he lived. No man seems able to escape the world that surrounds him, but some do it more easily than do others. Valéry was always within it. He could act upon it or retreat from it. These are the attractions we face when our concerns grow roots. What we say and do involves the quality of life we are forced to endure.

We find it extremely difficult to disagree with Valéry, who remarked that "there is no thinking person, however shrewd and experienced we imagined him to be, who can flatter himself that he is above this malaise" ("The European," 207). If *cette impression de ténèbres* doesn't completely destroy us in the labyrinths of melancholic despair, then the political event attempts to do the same. We find in it an event that captures the imagination, startles our imagination, and fascinates our willingness to act. We are citizens, children of a society whose responsibilities have not only turned inwardly but also outwardly. Valéry noted that "every essential thing in the world has been affected by the war, or more exactly, by the circumstances of the war" ("The European," 307). We become aware that political life is the canopy hanging over all of life. It covers every essential form of being even at those moments when the political seems to be inactive and distant from our concern, when it is like the sleeping lion which will hopefully sleep forever. This would give us pleasure. It would make us into fools.

Man is an adventurous being seeking to transfigure every aspect of life. From the beginnings, we found the paradise of Hesiod's natural society in which all living things share an immortality, and the absence of knowledge, which made living indistinguishable from nonliving. Man needed to experience material existence. He needed to erase immortality from his myth. He wanted knowledge and consciousness. They would open new visions and bring new dreams. These would bring with them illusions and fantasies delighting the human soul. Man wanted to invent heroes, to create myths about their preexistence. They were the models of his life. He adored and worshipped them. We wonder how life would be possible without dreams. We have a need to dream. We raise this need to a right and borrow a term from the philosopher Gaston Bachelard: *Le Droit de rêver*. This right to dream forged the attachment to the imagination. Man discovered that the imagination, together with reason, were his greatest assets. It sent him beyond the confines of household and community to dreams of conquest, to ventures into the seas, to the discovery of new lands. Valéry noted that "all our dreams are directed against all the given conditions of our finite existence. We are a zoological species that tends to transform the mode of existence, and we could draw up a table, a systematic classification of our dreams by considering each of them as attaching one of the original conditions of our life. There are dreams that defy gravity... some defy space and others time" ("The European," 310-11).

We should note that in the Greek texts dealing with the statesman, the citizen, and the constitution, we find no mention of history, of historical development, of man as an adventurer. Aristotle, who had a profound interest in biology, was bent upon classifications. He was a taxonomist. The statesman understood the form of political life because he had learned to identify every form of government, knowing that he had to discover the forms to which communities conformed. If we claim that man is a political being by nature, then what we must explore is nature and natural man. We don't escape our nature. We can easily disregard the accidental conditions which characterize our being. Heraclitus reminded us that character is fate, but we often remind him that character is nothing more than arbitrary attitudes and proclivities which we have assumed to be the fundamental conditions of our being. In other words, we reject the notion of nature as a clear and distinct idea, while at the same time, acknowledge the import of the term to avoid reducing everything to accidental and contingent manners of behavior.

Apart from the Aristotelian attitude lie the powers of the dream. The achievements which belong to dreams are the consequences of the idealism which is the foundation of the state. This foundation, we suppose, lies in the fact that man is not by nature a political being. He is by nature indifferent to political reality. He turns to it only as a protector for the realm of creativity in which morality, politics, economics are various and consequential expressions of his community with his fellow human beings.

In and out of community, men struggle with and for the dream. Valéry observed that "out of all these achievements, most, and the most astonishing and fruitful have been the work of a tiny portion of humanity, living in a very small area compared to the whole of the habitable lands. This privileged place was Europe; and the European man, the European mind was the author of these wonders" ("The European," 311). Europe is not defined only as the source of political reality, of the state, and the constitution, but on a deeper level, Europe is a culture, a profound expression of values, the birthland of poetry, theater, science, architecture, literature, etc. Its lands and its people gave rise to political and social orders which provided the protection and inspiration for men, and later women, of peculiar and inexplicable gifts. The state was not only classified as royal, democratic, aristocratic, but as an order synonymous with man as the creator of the arts and the sciences.

In the twentieth century, the central place of Europe and its extension into Africa, Asia, North and South America has been threatened. The centricity of Europe as the source of a unique civilization has faded into the belief that what is essential is the study of comparative civilization. The fundamental term is now *comparative*. It has become a gadfly term necessary for every serious thinker, necessary because it breaks the domination of European civilization and finds hidden sources which show origins in non-European places, among non-European peoples. I have the feeling that their attempts to challenge Europe can be ascribed to a feeling of revenge. If the European way is in many ways inimitable, then others are possible if this inimitable way is devalued in a world of comparative cultures. Every man has the right to an egotistic authority. He has the right to choose among the cultures with no fear of revealing a weak or inadequate aesthetic sense. Paradoxically, at the core of European thought lies the logic, the logic of rhetoric which makes this attitude possible. The European mind has been trained to find a logic by which we destroy Europe's cultural authority. This is the greatness of Europe.

A never-ending question comes forth again and again. It asks: What then is Europe? Qu'est-ce donc cette Europe? We don't only hear the question, but we listen to it. It communicates to us a reality that we are not often able to grasp. We reduce Europe to its history, to its art, its powerful and hegemonic states, to the greatness of its literature. Whatever we do, we find that we are inadequate. We have falsified. We are left with a distortion. Europe is always more than we describe and imagine. Europe "was a prey to a perpetual restlessness and search." It followed Odysseus and ventured into worlds of unknown possibilities. Its explorers, at first, chartered the coasts of unknown continents and then ventured into the seas and yet-to-be explored distant lands. Valéry said: "Every kind of exchange, every variety of problem multiplied and fermented in its midst; the means of life, knowledge and growth accumulated from century to century with extraordinary rapidity. Soon the difference between this portion of humanity and the rest of the world, as regards knowledge and power, became so great that it upset the equilibrium. Europe burst out of its borders, went out to conquer other lands....At home, Europe created the maximum of vitality, intellectual fruitfulness, riches and ambition" ("The European," 313).

Valéry, in 1945, in a lecture on Voltaire, spoke of the trembling of this Europe. This same Europe may be crumbling. The specter is there, but we can't rush to an imaginary end with gloom and declare the death of Europe. This is the work of Cassandra's children, but we can never be sure that they listened well. More often they hear what they need or want to hear. Cassandra has had unfaithful children. Those who are faithful are silent. They refuse to pick up the mantle of the prophet. They know that it is the gift of Medea.

Valéry has a long story to tell us about Europe. He tells us about a Europe which he knows well. It is a civilization which needs to be protected, nurtured, and believed in. Descriptions are never enough. They should become a faith, a value belonging to our soul, the source of our life. We need it to live. Without it we dissolve and even die. "Europe was a lively market," Valéry noted, "where all good and precious things were brought, compared and discussed...and changed hands. It was an Exchange where the greatest variety of doctrines, ideas, discoveries, and dogmas were *floated* and *quoted*, and rose or fell, and were the object of the most pitiless criticism and the blindest infatuation....The learning, the philosophies, the religions of ancient Asia came to nourish the ever alert minds that Europe produced in every generation; and this powerful machine transformed the more or less strange conceptions of the Orient –

sounded their depths and extracted from them their usable elements" ("The European," 314). In Valéry's descriptions we discover the uniqueness of Europe, the one that became embodied in him, the one from which he saw and heard the world. He was the European whose values made him the statesman of Europe. He was more than a French poet and essayist, a politician defending France's national interests, a thinker whose speculations led to learned articles, and a serious academic reputation, a member of the Academy. Valéry was a European figure representing and thinking for the serious public. We will return to this evaluation throughout our writings. It reveals the limitations of the intellectual, but also the bravery and insight demanded of a thinker who must be more than a thinker, more than a rationalist, who is a reasonable man.

Valéry stated that "a dynamic equilibrium has to be maintained between acquiring and preserving; but a more and more active critical sense attacks one of these tendencies or the other, pitilessly belaboring all favorite and established ideas, mercilessly testing and protesting both tendencies of that precariously kept balance" ("The European," 314). There seems to be an imbalance between our desire to discover the nature of our civilization, its constituent elements, and our sense of devotion to it. I can't imagine the will to study and to speculate about a nation and not discover that we have a love for it. I would say that we develop not only a loyalty for our nation, but for those others whose literature and arts we have come to know and appreciate. We develop also a commitment for both a concrete and abstract entity we call Europe-America. We conceive it as an expression of values we have learned to admire, even to love. It is at this point that we should extend our idea of Europe to include England and America both North and South. We agree fully with Valéry that America is the most formidable creation of the European mind. I am sure that if we turned this sentence about and spoke of Europe as the most formidable myth and symbol of the European mind, we would be approaching the truth. We might say that North America is Europe's Protestant expression, while Central and South America are its Catholic expression. Its rational expression fills all its expressions. We can hold to this general observation. In detail it slips through us, but enough is left to make it valid.

We search preliminarily for arching values which allow us to speak of the European mind, knowing that it embraces lands and seas, defying our definitions and surpassing our comprehension. I repeat what Valéry said about this mind: "Europe has been built up gradually like a gigantic city" ("The European," 314). This is now a city which has left colonies everywhere, ones that are so large and so powerful that they often suffocate and deeply subordinate the mother who brought them forth.

Valéry has carved for us meaningful descriptions of the European. They are beginnings awaiting and awakening expressions of his feelings and commitments. The statesman's voice goes beyond rationality, beyond the clarity of ideas, beyond the noble figures of Descartes and Leonardo da Vinci. It is the voice of the great rhetorician in whom both mind and feelings find the meaning of their existence and the future of their existence. We seek this voice in Valéry.

2

The Book That Defines Civilization

The road that may lead to our understanding or misunderstanding of the European, of Valéry as the sign and symbol of the European mind, is filled with dangers. There is no single ascent to the place of honor and no quick descent into its distortion. European civilization, if not definable, is, however, recognizable. There are broad characteristics that give us clues to this recognition. We have spoken of them. Valéry has spoken of them. The European "is caught between marvelous memories and immoderate hopes, and if sometimes he tends to pessimism, he cannot help noting that pessimism has produced certain works of art of the highest order. Instead of sinking into a mental void, he wrenches a song from his despair. Or sometimes he may wrench from it a tough and formidable will, a paradoxical incentive to action based on contempt for man, for life itself" ("The European," 315-16).

Why are we so deeply concerned about Valéry and the Europeans? We could dismiss our problem by denying that Europe has any particular or unique significance. We may claim that we are dealing only with a geographical area whose significance is now economic and technological rather than cultural. Culture is a private affair, having little to do with Europe's importance to the world. Can we say this about America, particularly North America? It seems to me that these are viable attitudes. The purpose of my thoughts about Paul Valéry may be of minor meaning. There are always little groups of scholars who like books about antiquated subjects. There will, hopefully, always be poets, essayists, storytellers, but these are limited to men and women who enjoy such works and establish societies to encourage them. There are always the universities which maintain their traditions of educating those who seek to learn and those who seek a gathering place for the materials necessary to their work.

If we accept this attitude and believe that there is an essential place for European culture, then we assume that there is a unique place for Valéry, for his statesmanship, and his values. This doesn't mean that we have elected him to be the measure and judge of what is Europe, of what is uniquely European, but we do believe that his stature and work have elevated him to that rare position of statesman. Others have been wise interpreters of European man, and the conditions in which he is living. We speak of Cioran or Ionesco, of Shestov or Camus, but they don't bring with them the enormity of embrace, the positivity of attitude, encompassing powers of the imagination and the intellect. No field is put aside. Valéry embraced Einstein as well as Bergson, Mallarmé and Voltaire. We don't want to list names when our purpose is clear. We want to show that no other thinker in our age found such deep interests in the sciences as he did in literature, and ultimately in political responsibility. One only has to read other thinkers to know how one-sided are their concerns, and in particular, their value judgments. Valéry opened texts which lighted every field of human knowledge he engaged, as well as the practical arts. He saw the multiple achievements of man, embracing those of the fingers and the intellect. We accord the honor of statesman to Valéry because of the fascination which comes to us not only from reading his works, but even more from reading the *Cahiers,* those startling texts which reveal the mind and the body, creating and reaching daily to the problems which face a thinking and doing man. It is a wonder beyond wonders to read through the *Cahiers* so beautifully organized by Judith Robinson Valéry in two volumes for the Bibliothèque de la Pléiade.

We have moved to broader paths and raised general problems. For the moment everything said is preliminary, and we return to the text. It is always the text that is vital. Valéry raised the question: "Mais qui donc est Européen?" (*Pléiade,* 1:1006). This concern with whom or what is European is asked from decade to decade. It must be asked. The mind and the feelings demand it. In fact, it appears naturally. What is of great concern are the answers which flow from it. I would venture to say that until 1945 the name Valéry was placed alongside the word *European.* In the following years, Europe had again to discover itself, but the shadow of Valéry is always present, awaiting the outcome of the various fancies which seem for the moment to capture and dominate Europe.

Valéry remarked that in seeking to comprehend what is European, certain elements need to be understood. He spoke of Rome as "the eternal model of organized and stable power" ("The European," 316). He then spoke of Christianity. It took all it could from Rome, and fixed its center there rather than in Jerusalem. It borrowed Rome's language. "A man born in Bordeaux could be a Roman citizen and even a magistrate and at the same time a bishop of the new religion. The same *Gaul* could be imperial prefect and in pure *Latin* write beautiful hymns to the glory of the Son of God born a Jew and a subject of Herod. There already, we have almost a complete European. A common law, a common God; one and the same temporal judge, and one and the same Judge in eternity" ("The European," 318). We reread these words and find images in them that surpass the imaginative capacities. All around us we see the crumbling of this commonality. The idea of Europe remains with us, but radically transformed and transfigured. We need not enumerate the changes which occurred from the rise of a national state to the Protestant Reformation and then to the age of reason and progress. They are here, these actualities. We are the expression of their existence, of their conflicts, and the conflicting ideologies which arose from them. We would find it difficult to believe that Europe was founded in both secular and religious beliefs. It is this amalgamation of the secular and the religious which gave Europe its unique place in the world. This didn't happen in either India or China. They didn't have their Machiavelli, their Calvin nor their Copernicus, and let us not forget Leonardo da Vinci and Montaigne.

We have no whimsical desire to compare the uniqueness of the European mind to any other mind or to compare the minds which exist together or are in conflict with each other. We search for similarity and subsequently for difference. It is similarity which makes difference possible. Valéry spoke of the unifying powers of Christianity which today seem more important for its denominations than the universal message brought to society. Valéry stated that "the new religion imposed self-examination. It may be said that it introduced Western man to that inner life which the Hindus had cultivated in their own way for centuries, and which the mystics of Alexandria in their way had also felt, recognized and studied" ("The European," 319). Religion, from century to century, was forced to consider questions which spoke of the purpose of life, of human destiny. It fought against the arbitrary and the chaotic. The faith of Thomas Aquinas struggled against the visions of John of Patmos just as today indifference struggles against belief, chaos is aroused against reason. Valéry put it well when in the first inscription for the Palais de Chaillot, he wrote:

> On The Passerby Depends
> Whether I Am Tomb Or Treasure House
> Whether I Speak Or Remain Mute
> It Rests With You Alone
> Friend Do Not Enter Without Desire.
>
> (*Occasions* [Princeton: Princeton
> University Press, 1970], vii)

If you can in any way be defined, then the definition belongs to man, to a being whose definition is a rejection of all definitions, who finds within himself rationality and imagination, metaphor and symbol. This is the being who addresses the Palais de Chaillot as either tomb or treasure, who chooses the word or silence. "Friend do not enter without desire." This speaks to those beings born in a geographical place called Europe. This speaks to a glaring and fundamental reality: every inhabitant of Europe is not a European. Every inhabitant enters the European community with particular and unique conditions, with a tradition, a history, and a religion. Each enters the realm of the Idea only because they choose to do so. They desire to take upon themselves the cloak of the European. They want to stand under the same canopy with others. Who knows what permits them to stand under this canopy? We are not satisfied with vague but encompassing ignorance. We have struggled to find out if our distance from Europe is so great that the separation destroys our unity. From the shores of North and South America we cry out, wanting to know, wanting to enter that community of thinking which we describe, but don't describe. We create a school, like that at Athens, and we decide to converse. We choose a master. We choose Paul Valéry and we begin to talk. We need to talk. He is the model. We listen to him and we absorb. There is joy in these conversations.

We were speaking of Christianity. We listen to Valéry's continuing evaluation. We are convinced that all problems are ultimately religious. "Christianity," Valéry remarked, "proposed to the mind the worst subtle, the greatest, and indeed the most fruitful problems. Whether it were a question of the value of a testimony, the criticism of texts, or the sources and guarantees of knowledge; of the distinction between faith and reason, and the opposition that rises between them, of spiritual and material power and their mutual conflict, the equality of men, the status of women – and how much else? Christianity educated and stimulated millions of minds, making them act and react, century after century" ("The European," 319). We read these lines and find in them that profound commitment to values that allows us to begin to understand what it means to be European. Suddenly, we see before us T.S. Elliot's *Murder in the Cathedral*. We hear the words of Thomas Becket, archbishop of Canterbury, and feel the pulse of Europe. We listen to the words of the third priest. Thomas has been murdered. The priest begins to speak, thanking God for giving us another saint in Canterbury. He speaks:

> Those who deny Thee could not deny. If Thou didn't exist; and
> their denial is never complete, for if it were so, they would not exist.
> They affirm that in living, all things affirm Thee in living; the bird
> in the air, both the hawk and the finch; the beast in the earth, both

the wolf and the lamb; the worm in the soil and the worm in the belly. (*Murder in the Cathedral*, Harvest/Harcourt Brace Jovanovich, 1935, 86)

We speak of the European mind. We speak of Christianity and what has flowed from it. Through the generations, it may have died as a dogmatic faith, but it lives fully and powerfully among us as an aesthetic and moral faith. It is a faith which belongs to the political realm. It separated clearly the "City of God" from the earthly city, the city of man. This brought with it a radical understanding of political life. This life was not labeled sinful, but necessary for the maintenance of order. This order had a natural history like that of slave-master to worker-owner. Recognizing the simplicity of our statements, we desire to make a single observation: the moral-political order is a natural human condition, just as the idea of freedom is faith.

Civilizations survive from generation to generation through repetition. They back up into their morality and die. Christianity has created some of the greatest problems facing the survival and purpose of humankind. It is tied to the problem of freedom. If, for example, we search for a text, we can do no better than read the *Spiritual Exercises* of Ignatius Loyola in which freedom of choice is the central concern of the novice. European civilization has no problem providing great thinkers and fascinating texts which are as meaningful today as they were generations ago. If we measure a civilization by its artistic, literary, and scientific greatness, we award the accolades to Europe. This is a civilization, like all others, that has lived a cruel and horrendous existence. It is a civilization of wars and hatreds. It advanced at the same time a sophisticated technology causing us to think of the destruction of the mind.

Christianity was not the only ingredient that was an essential factor. There was Greece and Rome. Without Greece and Rome, there is an imbalance. Valéry remarked that "what is missing is that marvelous transformation to which we owe, not the sense of public order, the cult of the city and of temporal justice, not even the depth of our consciousness...what is missing is rather that subtle yet powerful influence to which we owe the best of our intelligence, the acuteness and solidarity of our knowledge, also the clarity, purity and *elegance* of our arts and literature; it is from Greece that these virtues came to us" ("The European," 319).

When Valéry spoke of our debt to Greece, he pointed to the discipline of the mind, i.e., he pointed to the works of Aristotle, to his logical theories, to the syllogism, to a view of reality comprehended and organized through a process of classification. Classify, and you have properly understood reality. There was a Greece that Valéry considered.

There was another Greece with a different logic, the assumptions of the Sophists about whom Plato wrote several unfavorable dialogues. We remember Protagoras's statement that man is the measure of things that are and that are not. We recall this remark and with it we recall Plato's belief that God is the measure of all things. We wonder about every attempt to reduce Greek thinking to one thought or another, but it is important for us who draw our inspiration from Greek and Roman thought to realize that if we are attached to either the Stoics or the skeptics, we hold on only to one aspect of the classical tradition, the foundation of the European mind. We are aware that Valéry made a choice that drew him very close to the logical aspects of Aristotle's thinking and close to Plato's belief in the Idea. However correct these evaluations are, they point to something fundamental: to the belief that in the Greek and Roman basis of European civilization, in its theory of knowledge and beauty, we have a concept of thinking that has no parallel anywhere else in the world.

In reference to Greece, Valéry said: "To her we owe the method of thought that tends to relate all things to man, the complete man. Man became for himself the *system of reference* to which all things must in the end relate. He must therefore, develop all the parts of his being and maintain them in harmony as clear, and even as evident as possible. He must develop both mind and body. As for the mind, he must learn to defend himself against excesses and its reveries...by means of scrupulous criticism and minute analyses of its judgments" ("The European," 320). Valéry imagined a Greek world from which the science of geometry emerged. Europe was proclaimed to be the creator of science, although I wonder if the experimental sciences which Valéry adored were not more fully discovered in the cities of northern Italy, in their schools of medicine and law. No such anatomic experimentation took place in either Greece or Rome.

Valéry spoke of sciences as the search for the perfect theory, for the nondebatable truth. "To develop science as we have it," he said, "a relatively perfect model had to be established, a first work had to be set up as an ideal, representing every form of precision, every proof, every beauty, every solidity, and which should once and for all, define the very concept of science as a pure construct, free of every consideration but the edifice itself. Greek geometry was that incorruptible model" ("The European," 321). When I read these words, understanding seemed to mix with misunderstanding. I thought of the magnificence of Valéry's constructs, how passionately he searched for scientific truth and precision in the art of thinking, of experimentation, but I also felt the dreamlike impossibilities which confronted every truth seeker. I remembered those words: "scrupulous criticism and minute analyses of its judgments" and I wondered if these words were not fantasies. I didn't want to think of them as illusions. I knew that I could not judge. I knew only that some things had to be true. There would be no possible way of living in the world if gravitation didn't make it possible. Concepts develop from concepts. Experimentations follow experimentations with variations and changes which baffle but excite our thinking, stimulating it to newer and more novel experimentations and analyses. I think of Valéry, the poet, the essayist, in the midst of scientific theory, following it in details, writing his speculations in his *Cahiers.* What sort of poet and essayist will emerge from such a mind? The poet of identity.

"Think," Valéry said, "what an innovation was that almost ceremonial form, which in its general outline is so beautiful and pure. Think of that magnificent division of the Mind into separate moments, that marvelous order in which each act of reason is clearly placed, clearly distinct from the others. It reminds us of the structure of a temple, a static assemblage whose elements are all visible and all declare their functions" ("The European," 322). In this sublime architectural structure, there are no sophists and no rhetoricians. Plato chased away the poets, the falsifiers of reality, from his republic, fearing the distortion which they brought to truth in their words. Valéry chased the theories of argumentation from his thinking, fearing the doubts and ultimately the chaos which they might bring to the purity of science. Science alone laid the foundation for thinking. He saw in it the way to explore the depths of the human mind, granting it its autonomy, refusing to allow it to be hindered by falsities flowing from traditions, from the events of everyday life, from the politics of conflict and the sophistical instrumentalities of argumentation that sought to prevent truth through the destructive powers of doubt.

In a further analysis and evaluation of the Greek epistemological achievements, Valéry enumerated details of this accomplishment. He spoke of such instrumental terms as: "*definitions, axioms, lemmas, theorems, corollaries, porisms, problems...*that is to say, the mechanism of the mind made visible, the very architecture of intelligence drawn to a plan – the temple erected to Space by the Word, yet a temple that can rise to infinity" ("The European," 322). If we read these descriptions again, we discover that they are not necessarily related to particular sciences but to all human work. In fact, we may say that this belief in scientific methodology expressed the belief which each creative man found necessary to promote the rationality of science. Rationality promoted clarity and preciseness. It makes us conscious of the powers of the human mind which we are just beginning to comprehend. Valéry struggled to make us conscious of our responsibility, not only to thinking per se, the process by which an object comes into existence. We need to be aware of the processes of thinking, of the meaning of a vocabulary which can express adequately the working of the mind. Each of us must be a logician. Logic is the preparation for thinking and doing. If we assume that this is true, then we can say that "every race and land that has been successfully Romanized, Christianized, and, as regards the mind, disciplined by the Greeks, is absolutely European" ("The European," 322). It seems to be broad enough a description to force us to agree with it. We know that with such a generality we are quite safe. But to be European can also mean a possible, or perhaps impossible, amalgamation of the general and the particular. Historical life brings with it anti-European feelings, the search for a non-European existence, a struggle to prevent the European from becoming part of individual existence. The individual is not only an expression of the generalization realizing its reality, but it is also an opposition attempting to destroy generalization.

We have spoken of three characteristics: the Roman, the Greek, and the Christian. We have sought to define the European with them. The various European cultures have undergone perhaps one or two of these characteristics, but rarely have they gone through all of them. The influences have been more or less substantial. Valéry absorbed the European mind. Our imagination follows his mind, knowing that it has profoundly undergone these characteristics. He describes them as if he believes in them. We are sure that his descriptions are his beliefs. They are confirmed by his commitments. We follow him not only because we accept the descriptions, but also because we feel that in them Valéry found the articles of his faith. Was he a Christian? He was a man of deep spiritual convictions. He could write convincingly of the work of Henri Brémond (1865-1933), whose *L'Histoire littéraire du sentiment religieux* is of monumental importance in France for every student of the history of religion. Valéry wrote a beautiful, as if inspired, preface, "Cantiques spirituels," to *Les Cantiques spirituels de St. Jean de la Croix* (1641). Was he Roman? He was a Roman in his appreciation of order, of the law which Rome brought to the world. He appreciated the republic and empire, a place for the receptivity not only of Greek thought, but also the literature of Rome; of Terence, Lucian, Ovid, Tacitus, and Pliny. He respected the Greek in his adoration of architecture, of form in every possible mode. He was Greek in his devotion to logic, to the classifications of methodologies. How could a thinker not admire Greece, not find in his studies of Heraclitus or Parmenides the problems which have always plagued the human mind and created, in particular, the European mind?

Valéry made this quite clear. He remarked that "there is a certain trait, then, quite distinct from race, nationality, and even language which unites the countries of the West and Central Europe, making them alike.

The number of notions and ways of thought they have in common is much greater than the number of notions we have in common with an Arab or a Chinese....In short, there is a region of the globe that is profoundly distinct from all others, from the human point of view" ("The European," 323). In spite of every attempt to destroy the idea of Europe, despite attempts to ignore the idea, the name bears in it a unifying power that seems to be invincible. From its ashes new and more novel forms emerge. The older idea becomes renewed with a greater and greater vigor. This optimism demands a pessimism by which everything is thrown into doubt. Europe can be destroyed. It can be crushed by a radical skepticism which eliminates every possible value, that leaves Europe a hardened shell which has lost the internal substance. We have that dreadful feeling that events occur long before we recognize them. Hegel taught us this. The thought hangs about as if it were a shadow that can't be swept away. We speak of Europe, but again and again we must be conscious of what we do and say. Civilizations are mortal. They die or fade into others. Valéry spoke of their mortality and has left us with an awareness which seems never to have faded away. The mortality is caught within us.

In the luxuries of hope and dream, Europe remains confident of her survival, but this survival, which is also that of North and South America, has to be pragmatically accepted. Today we can repeat with Valéry that "Europe still greatly outweighs the rest of the world. Or rather, it is not so much Europe that excels but the European Mind, and America as its formidable creation" ("The European," 323). Civilization doesn't only exist where this mind prevails, but it exists in it. It excels when this crucial moment arrives and the internal finds expression in the external, or when what is internal becomes external. We speak these words easily. We feel them with difficulty. The difficulty grows as we immerse ourselves in the history of the European mind following Valéry's death in 1945. Europe began to reexperience what had occurred. What was continuing to occur was an aggravated state of the past. Hitler and Mussolini were dead. Stalin remained. We didn't comprehend the horrors which were now to appear. They had appeared. The poets, the writers made us see more fully, more deeply what had happened and what was happening. How long, we wondered, could Europe endure the onslaught of moral decrepitude?

At the end of the article, Valéry observed that the source of Europe's development, this astonishing superiority "is obviously the quality of the individual man, the average quality of *Homo europaeus*. It is remarkable that the European is defined not by race or language, or customs, but by his aims and the amplitude of his will" ("The European," 323). We remember that Valéry wrote this text in 1922. We are discussing it seventy-seven years later. We can't escape the fateful reality of time. It weighs upon us. It has become a fate. We seek no escape. We wonder if we can evaluate the changes that have occurred. We can't but we try. We hope that what we say is persuasive. The world war lasted six years but deeper than that is the moral revolution, the disappearance of both the Judaic and the Christian tradition, the reduction of religion to the private realm, a reduction built on the walls of a terrifying orthodoxy formed no longer in learning but in exclusivity. The voyages which this century have taken are those leading to concentration camps, to slave labor camps. We read in our novelists and poets different ways of speaking about the same things. One of our great literary figures, Jorge Semprun, begins his novel *Le Grand Voyage* (1963) with these words: "There is the cramming of bodies into the boxcar, the throbbing pain in the right knee. The days, the nights. I force myself to try to count the days, to count the nights. Maybe that will help me see clearly. Four days, five nights. But I must have counted wrong, or else some of the days must have turned into nights. I have a surplus of nights, more nights than I can use" (*The Long Voyage*, Penguin Books, 1977, 9). I cite these words only to indicate the course of European civilization filled with racial hatreds, civil wars, and intellectual chaos.

We find it difficult to speak of Europe without also speaking of North and South America. These are lands of infinite possibilities. These are the lands of the future whose achievements in science and literature will mark again and again the uniqueness of the mother lands of the continent and the British Isles. In 1938, Valéry wrote a piece for the Mexican literary journal *Síntesis* under the title "America: A Projection of the European Mind" (L'Amérique, projection de l'esprit européen). He said that "whenever my thoughts turn too black and I despair of Europe, I can find some hope only in thinking of the New Continent. To the two Americas, Europe has sent her message, the communicable creation of her mind, the most positive things she has discovered, and in short, whatever was least likely to deteriorate from convergence and separation from its normal circumstances. A veritable 'natural selection' has taken place, extracting from the European mind those of its products having universal value, while whatever was too conventional or too historical in content was left behind in the Old World" ("America: A Projection of the European Mind," in *History and Politics*, 330-31). Valéry had linked Europe and America in such a way that there is a continuous movement from one to the other. We are crossing the seas and returning over the seas. We move quickly in one direction and find that we have been moving simultaneously in the other. The voyages have created not only technological links but cultural ones. We hear from each other constantly, daily, hourly, and even more often. We wonder if what we have linked has common values, ones that not only unite us commercially and technologically, but also culturally. The Second World War left many gaps in our unity. Nations struggle for their own survival.

Europe not only crossed the Atlantic, it penetrated India, China, the Philippines, and Japan. The Jesuits brought Christianity to the civilizations of the East, struggled to make translations and show the similarities of the faith. They did it successfully, at times unsuccessfully. The most significant idea that Valéry offered us was the idea of remembrance. The Americas will be the depositories of the European remembrance, in libraries, in universities. "The memory of our labors, the names of our greatest men will not be as though they had never been, and that here and there in the New World there will be minds to give a second life to some of the marvelous creations of unhappy Europe" ("America," 331). I wonder if, speculatively, Valéry noted the possibility of a Europe perishing or withering away, or if this was a presentiment which he took seriously. He thought that "our cities, museums, monuments and universities would be destroyed" in the furies of a scientifically waged war. His visions are not merely apocalyptically imagined, but emerge from a frightening, serious dream of the future of Europe.

I would like to end this chapter by citing from one that Valéry wrote for a book. The chapter was called "The Physical Aspects of A Book" (Le Physique du livre). The book was published in 1945. I recalled this chapter. It is particularly relevant to an understanding of the power of the book, a book that is civilization. Groups have been called "the people of the book." A poet, recently deceased, Edmond Jabes, was labeled the poet of the book, the book created in the desert from the experiences of the Israelites. We heard the words of Valéry. They touched us deeply: "A Book is a singular object, an open and shut thing which changes its nature completely in that simple act. I open it: it speaks. I close it and it becomes a thing to be looked at. Thus more than anything else in the world, it resembles a man. At first approach, a man is his form and color; next his voice strikes us, and finally his voice is transformed into a mind that mingles with our own" ("The Physical Aspects of a Book," in *Aesthetics* [New York: Pantheon, 1964], 212).

The wonder of the book lies not only in its production – this is indeed a wonder – but in its transformative and transfigurative powers. The book emerges from the soul of a people. It speaks to that soul. I think of Homer, of Dante, of Cervantes, of Shakespeare, of Rabelais, of Swift. Names come from all corners and I leave it to the reader to make his own list, the list of life. The book reveals to us how easily it can be set aside, burned and mutilated. It can be scorned and mocked. It and its companions make wonderful and frightful barn fires. They bear witness to our wisdom and foolishness, but above all, they reveal the workings of the mind, the great creations of the human species.

The book follows us. It leads us. We go with the book. There is no other reason for it to be a book. It is an object with weight and size, with color and form, but it is and is not a book. We lift the book from the books. Each of us is given or takes a few books in our lifetime. We read few books, even fewer are reread. Few remain with us. Few are those we need as companions without whom we diminish our reality. The miracle of Europe is that it brought forth from itself a people of the book, those who found in the book the precious words of man's indefinable creativity. For ages other men sought to destroy these lovers of books. Often they succeeded. Often they failed. The people of the book don't increase in numbers. They don't decline. They remain eternally the same, a model for the others, a resistance for the cowardly, a strength for the weak, a word for the silent. I think often of the book. I visit it and we talk. The book has various tales to tell, various struggles to reveal, many stories to give to us relating the history of man's most precious gift. The book has a history among the human race. We want to learn its history, a history which began with Homer, a history we must learn. There are stories which have not yet been told. We listen for these among the silent whiteness which accompanies and forms our words. It is the whiteness of silence which shows us the blackness of the letters. We not only see them. We also hear them. We imagine them and we are transfigured by them. The page of the book startles us. It says quietly to us: This is man's creation. Suddenly another voice says: This is a divine creature. Each looks upon the other in quiet contemplation. They know that truth has two faces, each striving to ignore the other, but unable to. Each writes a book. They walk together peacefully, each thinking to itself that its rival is only a partial truth. Happy in this realization, each yearns one day to conquer the other.

Valéry's view turns to the construction of the book. It is the process of binding which attracts him. We are greatly attracted by the art of binding. The book becomes an object of respect and love. The usable paperback is easily discarded. The book is a work of art, held reverentially in our hands, touched delicately, and admired sensuously. In this respect, the book is the finest mark of our civilization's achievement. Valéry related that "for several years in my youth, I was preoccupied by the problem of the ornament. Nothing gave me more food for reflection than the spontaneous appearance, everywhere, of this very primitive form of production, developing like richly diversified vegetation...and changing with climate and race; while concomitantly the mysterious instance for representing being and things, no less ancient and inborn, dating in fact from prehistoric times, emerged and asserted itself in wonderful pictures of men and animals" ("The Physical Aspects of a Book," 213).

We are conscious of a desire to find pleasurable and attractive things with which we will find the unknown corners of our life. We invent things to amuse ourselves, we take pleasure in novelties. It seems as if all that we do is to push back the incoming waves of boredom which overflow our being like an incurable disease. Our struggle is endless and often fruitless. It is this boredom that stimulates our creativity. If we do well, we owe this boredom a debt. If we do it badly, we owe the boredom nothing. We have been overcome. It suffocated us. Boredom is a challenge we take seriously. It is the creator of the arts and sciences. It forces us to turn to conditions we have never questioned but repeated continuously. We need to be driven to change, to the consciousness of endless variations and possibilities. These are often exciting and demanding. In them live the vitality of a culture or a civilization.

In the unopened book lies the beginnings of creativity, possibilities which, for the moment, we have not acknowledged. Valéry spoke of "the world of symmetry, contrast, gradation, chiaroscuro, modulation and resemblance – a vibrant, self-sufficient world in which desire can create what it lacks, provided only..." ("The Physical Aspects of a Book," 214). The book is already being created. Desire seeks to understand what's been given and how this given belongs to our being. It belongs to us as a book that can only be repeated. Homer lives in us for the length of our years. He passes from one form to another. The years bring us changing views of Homer, ones that challenge our imagination but never conquer it. We must be stimulated to read or reread the book. It calls to us and we reply. We can turn away but we don't. The book gained power over us. We are its possession more than we are its possessor. The book is the mystery of our being. We live to discover it, but we often despair. This book is unconquerable. It bears us through the ages. We accept it. We are responsible for it. We are created in it. We look at it and we say: Here I am.

3

Art and Politics

The book is a political reality. It fears powers that go far beyond its immediate substance. Valéry noted that "a visible object which makes us aware, first, that *it might not have* existed (since its non-existence would have meant no vital loss), and secondly, that it could not have been other than it is: such an object we declare to be *beautiful*" ("The Physical Aspects of a Book," 215). I speak of the metamorphosis of the book. I have read the book. I have spoken of it. I have held it in my hands and admired it. I remembered that a little figure arose from it and began to speak to me. The atmosphere was dreamlike, but the conversation was clear. I felt as if the book had become a person wanting to speak with me. Characters had come forth from the book. They were alive. They were no longer the subjects of the author. They were free. They no longer felt bound to their creator. I wondered about this freedom from the creator. It made not only a literary, but also a political, statement: No man, not even a literary character, was the tool of its maker. I was made. I had freedom. The character could turn upon its maker. He could even destroy him. Books bring fear to kings and dictators, to ideologies which are inseparable from their creations. The book is a source of beauty or ugliness. It leads both the timid and the strong to places they have never imagined. Books are often filled with poetry. They delicately guide the reader to the beautiful and sublime. Books separate people from each other. They reach out to different souls, bringing them closer and closer to each other, forcing them to exercise their capacities to will and to feel. "Artists," Valéry observed, "are fallible, indeed the most fallible of all makers" ("The Physical Aspects of a Book," 215). It is this fallibility that makes the work of art a potential political work.

Fallibility reveals political mortality. The totalitarian is not fallible. Orthodoxy is not fallible. Fallibility is a sin. Who then is fallible? Valéry told us that the artists are the most fallible, but we wonder how large a canopy this fallibility covers. Valéry remarked that "everything that shows a happy result to an uncertain and even inexplicable thing, puts the idea of automation further from the mind" ("The Physical Aspects of a Book," 215). We wonder if the book is an aspect of fallibility, if it could be written and conceived only in a society that recognizes the rights of fallibility. The infallible individual writes no book. He needs no book. He is the book. His infallibility has only to be perfected in the mechanism of action. He smiles at his automatism. He takes pleasure in it. The fallible man fears his lack of precision. His mechanism may work poorly. He may be scorned and taunted. Exile is the only escape. We easily accept the fallible individual. We fear the infallible one. He causes us to despair. We feel fright in his presence. Our being is threatened. It weakens. Its unity is shattered. The loss of given truth shocks our intellect, shatters our feelings. We hide, become melancholic. We take comfort in darkness. We live in corners. We find them pleasurable. The light startles us. It reveals too much. Too many eyes are focused upon us. Too many ears surround us. We are haunted by fearful images and insights. They are beastly. The imagination fills us with exaggerations and unhappy wonders. We have been distorted by the infallible messages which we have badly learned that fall from our mouths comically. Laughter covers our anxiety, but it doesn't hide our chaos, our need for security. We would surrender everything for security. We would sell our souls if there were purchasers. We cost so little that there are few buyers. The fallible soul is in search of a fallible land. There alone he speaks and forms the oddities of his craft, and his intellect.

Fallible belief has a close alliance with the unexpected, the unknown, and the ambiguous, but above all, it is perplexity that dominates the mind, longing for clarity and definition. The mind needs obstacles. Clarity and precision plague its need for complexity and a happy disorder. We long for the puzzle that we don't easily master, for the confusion which we can't quickly resolve. In each of us there is a point at which we surrender, throw in the towel, and let others resolve our difficulties. Freedom becomes the main obstacle. We wish it away. The book is freedom, but it can be easily discarded. It is remembered. It lies upon us like a shadow having no movement. We may despise this freedom, but we love and respect it. It is the source of our life, but we don't control it. We are not the master. We are the slave. It draws us toward new directions. We don't go easily. We hesitate and resist. We prefer the Golden Calf. Moses speaks too cryptically. We follow him too uneasily. We await the priests, the interpreters, to make his words palatable. Freedom is terrifying. We are lovers of leaders. They afford us the daily habits of life. We want little else. The book that lies alone is a danger. Visions and images arise from it. It contains the imagination of

John of Patmos. We want to be overwhelmed. We need a purpose for our lives. We see our anxieties fly away. We walk without burden. His book has released us, and we smile contentedly. The Apotcrypha has a double face. It brings us our burdens. It takes them away. In some mysterious way we are determined to follow one path or the other. We believe that we have heard the word which showed us the direction. We followed.

Turning again to the binding of the book, Valéry noted that "in all the cases I have mentioned, the artist-binder has been concerned solely with the exterior of the book; there is no relation between this body and the soul: once the volume is opened and begins to speak, the binding ceases to exist" ("The Physical Aspects of a Book," 218). The binding will always exist. The book will change perpetually. It has become thinking, a grand mixture of black and white spaces. Thought will penetrate all sorts of readers. It will be discussed in the marketplace, in the newspapers, around political leaders. The book is a political instrument, arousing public opinion, dividing the public into opposing groups. They will struggle among themselves, take up arms, and sacrifice their lives. The book is, at times, revolutionary. It cuts history into a before and an after. This the poet, the ideologist, and the scientist can do. The book can do all these things and even others. We don't know what other consequences the book can have. We live in wonder and amazement. We are fascinated by those who have always known that books must be reluctantly read. The book doesn't find a home in every soul. In many it is distorted. In others it is welcomed, but it dies of boredom. In those dwellings where it grows and develops, it is honored, repeated, and remembered. The book has a life that few of us can adequately trace. Its life encompasses our civilization and overwhelms us. We leave it to each individual to discover the meaning of the book. We cannot do otherwise. We do this with love and despair, but we remember that the book is fallible, that we are fallible, that all that we experience is fallible. We take some comfort in Valéry's words: "This preposterous and unauthentic striving for authenticity could only have been thought desirable at a time when taste was corrupt" ("The Physical Aspects of a Book," 219). I shake my head in wonder and reply: Perhaps! Has there ever been a time when taste was not corrupt, when in its magnificence it joins "the lie to the truth"?

The mind, in its powers of play, revealed to us a simple truth which Valéry expressed when he said, at the end of his introduction to Baudelaire's edition of Poe's *Eureka*: "In the Beginning Was the Fable." We add to this a cunning and sharp remark made in one of his most delightful essays, "A Fond Note on Myth": "The mind goes one better than Nature, not only does it create, as she does, but on top of that it *appears* to create. It joins the lie to the truth" ("A Fond Note on Myth," in *History and Politics*, 40). Valéry spoke of this relationship from a literary point of view. The lie is a wonder? a breeder of illusion carefully laced with crumbs of truth. How ingenious is the interlacing, the joining and weaving. The lie has always had magical power. The words of the serpent echo all about us. We hear the serpent's words: You shall be like God. This is the lie that has driven man mad, that has given him utopian visions and hopes, that has filled his dreams with hopes that refuse to come true. The lie is the creator of politics. The statesman uses it craftily. He slides it into truth but doesn't destroy falsehood. The lie enhances truth, covering its ornamental beauty. The lie knows that nothing escapes its grasp. Its powers are endless. Valéry knew that "there is no discourse so obscure, no tale so old, or remark so incoherent that it cannot be given a meaning. There is always some supposition to give meaning even to the strongest language" ("A Fond Note on Myth," 40). The lie is more than a supposition. It is the companion of truth, living together with it, and infinitely combining the most subtle and malicious minds, knowing well the weavers of the art.

In a recently published interview with the Romanian novelist and short-story teller Norman Manea, the question of the lie came up. Manea said that "the lie is man's most extraordinary invention. Between its benign game and its maleficent perversity, a vast human terrain opens up, an abyss which, at times, we fear to scrutinize" (*Salmagundi,* [Winter 1997]: no. 13, 104). We wonder why the lie came so quietly into man's story. We would escape an answer if we stated that it was consubstantial with man's nature, dwelling with, and in, man's goodness and rationality. This seems again to be inadequate. We wonder why the lie needs to dwell with any other substance. The lie is autonomous. But again this autonomy would be difficult to explain without believing in the demiurge, creator of a fallen world. The lie confuses us. In this respect, in this confusion, we discover the lie. In a text of Saint Paul to the Colossians, it states: "Stop lying to one another, now that you have discarded the old nature with its deeds, and have put on the new nature which is being constantly renewed in the image of its Creator and brought to know God" (Col. 3:9-11, New English Bible).

We always take Paul seriously when we search for clear theological statements, but we wonder if the new nature is not the fundamental lie of our civilization, the belief that human nature absorbs the divine nature, presuming that both natures are one, or that the sinless nature is absorbed in the sinful and redeems it. They may not be one. They may be eternally separated from each other, in eternal conflict. If men were to believe this inseparability dogmatically, there would be no possibility for another expression, for doubt or ambiguity. This is the model for every identification of spirit and matter. Where this identification is believed, the totalitarian world reappears. Man is convinced again and again that the divine-human separation can be overcome. Let's play politics. Identify with a leader, with a charismatic one, if available. I search for a class to hate or a group to disdain as being below the human and thus inferior. I join a party or a movement and look to it for rewards. I feel as if I have the right color, the right religion, and the right politics. I serve my nation. I begin to march, to set fires, and to shout slogans. I have become a crude political being. In fact, I have become a nonpolitical being. I have become a mobster, whether I am physically active or not. If not, I send money and convince my friends to do the same. I might not read the sacred book, but I make sure that my wife and children do. I need them to hate evil religions and races. Other books I burn or I watch them burn. I keep my old nature in its corrupted form. I identify my new nature with the leader and the party, with our utopia built on racial and ideological purity and the clarity of definitions. Even our science has been purified and expresses the feeling of the people. The old classes are gone. They have become ashes. We have joyfully scattered them to the winds. The truth has been separated from the lie. The lie is free to give itself its true name. It calls itself the truth of truths. We created our myths, having declared rationality dead. We don't want its light to uncover the mysteries and inadequacies of our myths. Let our myths now be sacred and untouchable. Valéry noted that "whatever perishes from a little more clarity is a myth. Under the vigorous eye, under the repeated and convergent blows of questions and categories with which the alert mind is armed at all points, myths die and a fauna of vague things and vague ideas wither away" ("A Fond Note on Myth," 41). History, Valéry reminded us, is a long series of nightmares, incoherences, and ambiguities. What would they be without the rationality to reduce and organize them, "retain some and discard others, decide their values and allow us to go beyond them....The whole history of thought is nothing but the play of an infinite number of small nightmares of great consequence, whereas in sleep we have great nightmares of very short, very slight consequence" ("A Fond Note on Myth," 42).

We are convinced that rationality is our savior and many among us contribute to this fiction. It is a lie stimulated by the ingenious qualities of the demons. The lie is encompassed in rationality. There it seeks to dominate its powers, to refine and nurture them. Rationality is not an easy victim. Its ways and forces have been developed for generations and if the lie has made inroads, it has done it slowly and hesitantly. We wonder if the lie is not at the core of human nature. Man adores life. He dances excitedly about the golden calves, millions and millions of these calves. He draws them into himself. He speaks of them when sitting down, when standing up, when thinking and playing. We are myth makers. We draw the events of our lives into myths and send them out among our neighbors and friends. We are prepared to listen to every kind of myth, even to those which speak of the goodness of man. We hear the words of leaders and believe them. We are incredible believers of things we know, and know not. This is a proclivity which comes naturally. We know of the great art of rhetoric, of its capacities to convince and persuade. Secretly we are little rhetoricians, making or repeating speeches we have heard and which appeal to us. Valéry noted that "there are so many myths in us, that are so familiar a part of us, that it is almost impossible to pick out clearly in our minds anything that is not a myth. We cannot even speak of them without mythifying, and am I not at this moment creating a myth about myth, in reply to the caprice of a myth?" ("A Fond Note on Myth," 42).

If myth is in us, and drifts toward us from all directions, we feel as if we are the consequence of ideas, ideologies, and beliefs which we never sought to create, but do create ceaselessly. The philosopher Ernst Cassirer wrote a book titled *The Myth of the State* (1946) which revealed the depth of our captivity to myth. Myth easily becomes a devastating aspect of our culture. It transfigures history into divine tales which become truths leaving no room for doubts. We are delighted with myths when they give us aesthetic pleasure, when we are already convinced that they float above the realm of rationality and reasonableness. It is a creative realm in which the imagination indulges its fancy for metaphors and metamorphosis. Divinity playfully seeks the divine human form while man lovingly hopes to be divine and play god. We observe these games with theatrical delight. We walk away pleased. The entertainment has been good, comical, and filled with laughter. The divine and the human are proper companions, knowing how to flow into each other without friction. When friction does arise, we watch it with absorbing seriousness. We watch the jealousies of Artemus and Aphrodite. We are fascinated by those who are caught between them. We create Faustian myths of love. We sing them. We compose poetry. We write plays. "Remember," Valéry observes, "that tomorrow is a myth, that the universe is one; that numbers, love, the real and the infinite...that justice, the people, poetry...the earth itself are myths!...I forgot to mention the whole of the past....All history is made up of nothing but thoughts to which we attribute the essentially mythical value of representing what was....Hardly are our backs turned, hardly are we out of sight, before opinion makes of us whatever it can!" ("A Fond Note on Myth," 43).

The myth is a literary form. Its relationship to knowledge is obscured, although present. There is a relationship. There is a mirage of a bridge leading from one to the other. A mirage is only a vague vision. It bears in it illusion. Truth has no claim upon us, no claim greater than myth. There is, however, a serious danger lying in the myth. Man joins the political lie to it. The myth and the lie become one. The myth was free of the struggle between the lie and the truth. It was imaginative fiction exercising the powers of the creative imagination, revealing to man the wonders of his freedom. In these wonders, man discovered the self, the free self. The myth induced man to create in metaphorical language, to realize that the world about and in him shares truth with discussion, with possibility. Truth, like love or righteousness, is a human activity. One day it occurred to some men to fill myth with truth, making it impossible to distinguish one from the other. Suddenly, we discovered that myth came from the heavens, that it was a shroud in which truth appeared. Men developed racial, national, biological, scientific myths and proclaimed them to be truth. Myth, however, is never truth. Forms of government, economic, political, and social theories have come down to us from the heavens where truth had again lodged itself. It had been thrown down to the earth. There is a beautiful Midrash telling us of God throwing truth to earth: "He took truth and cast it to the ground" (*The Book of Legends,* Sefer Ha-Agadah [New York: Schocken Books, 1992], 13-46). This statement is repeated in Ps. 85:12: "Truth springs up from the earth, justice looks down from heaven." A terrifying violence has occurred. The myth has again invaded the heavens, and with truth, demanded a place with justice. The myth discovered Pandora's box. The dictators stand about and gather what they need. God has retreated and hidden himself from the world. The battle is joined between justice and mythical truth. This is the politics of our century, the politics of the myth that has become the truth.

Valéry observed with frightening depth that "everywhere, in every place and every period of civilization, in every discipline and every relationship...the false supports the true, the true takes the false as its ancestor, its cause, its author, its origin and end, without exception or remedy – and the true engenders the false from which in turn it requires to be engendered. All antiquity, all causality, all principles of things are fabulous inventions and obey simple laws" ("A Fond Note on Myth," 43-44). We cite these words because in some way they make us giddy. The expression *le faux supporte le vrai* is at first difficult for us to use. We would rather believe that the false supports the false and the true supports the true. It is difficult to imagine the one supporting the other but a more careful observation and analysis causes us to see a dependence and a support that is necessary from the moment we realized that truth belongs to the earth as well as the false. They both crawl upon the ground seeking survival and life. They learn from each other. Their conditions are the same, but the consequences they draw from these conditions are profoundly different. From the view of the political, a dualism is essential. What we call the enemy is the negation of what we have labeled the positive. What the other proclaimed the positive is for us the negation. We must fight for the victory of either the one or the other. The struggle demands unconditional surrender. We accept nothing less. We proclaim a return of the truth to the heavens. We join it with righteousness. We condemn to death all who accept this union.

Valéry posed this question: "What should we be without the help of that which does not exist?" He answered the question directly: "Very little. And our unoccupied minds would languish if fables, mistaken notions, abstractions, beliefs, and monsters, hypotheses and the so-called problems of metaphysics did not people with beings and objectless images our natural depths and darkness" ("A Fond Note on Myth," 44). We wonder if it is against fancies that we are forever struggling, ever seeking a truth behind an appearance, even convincing ourselves that there are such truths and they must be discovered. If such truths exist, they must not be discovered. How could the undiscoverable be discovered? We would cease thinking and begin repeating. We would cease loving our creations and begin adoring them. We would reduce the myth to a psychological insight usable for a statistic. We would reduce it to a sociological fact necessary to explain the ingredients of a functioning society. We leave myth to poetic act, to an indescribable and unknowable freedom, the act that is filled with beauty, the act that elevates us beyond all other beings in creativity. I know also of evil myths. They have grown powerfully in our century, perverted and distorted by evil men. They created evil nations and ideologies.

The myth weeps eternally for the damages that have been done to it. There is nothing and no one to dry its tears. The wounds that have been inflicted do not heal. They fester. No person dares to approach the myth. A disease radiates from it. We wonder how to cleanse this wound and take back the creativity of the myth. We have pondered in pain the loss we have suffered. Remember the council of gods at which Athena spoke, having witnessed the suffering of Odysseus in Calypso's house. I recall the scene.

> As Dawn rose up from bed by her lordly mate Tithonus,
> bringing light to immortal gods and mortal men,
> the gods sat down in council, circling Zeus
> the thunder king whose power rules the world.
> Athena began, recalling Odysseus to their thoughts,
> the goddess deeply moved by the man's long ordeal,
> held captive still in the nymph Calypso's house.
> (*The Odyssey*, trans. Robert Fagles, v. 152).

We yearn for a council. We long for the voice of Athens. We hope that our myth will be preserved, and the evil which has been done to it can be washed away. We listen but there are no sounds. There is a painful and terrifying silence, and I recall the weeping myth. I know how deeply Valéry loved the myth and longed for her presence, how deep was his despair when the myth became the truth and now was worshipped and came down into the realm of man's perversion. We hoped for a message, an "imperial message," that has been sent, but has not arrived and may never arrive. We can only dream that such a message has been sent. Kafka reminded us that we must sit by our windows and dream. Odysseus was more fortunate. The goddess convinced Zeus.

> With those words, Zeus turned to his own son Hermes.
> You are our messenger, Hermes, sent on all our missions.
> Announce to the nymph with lovely braids our fixed decree:
> Odysseus journeys home – the exile must return.
>
> *
>
> So Zeus decreed and the giant-killing guide obeyed at once.
> (*The Odyssey*, v. 153).

The political life of Valéry, who was so conscious of the distortion and perversion of the myth, grew endlessly with the realization that the myth had been destroyed, that it was now shattered, that destructive forces had arisen with enormous powers and had revered a divine act. Truth had to be thrown out of heaven and given to the earth. The gods of the earth and their puppets threw truth back to the heavens with such force that God hid himself, his angels followed him and truth dwelled again in the heavens. Myth no longer recognized itself. It grew silent. Others now used it at their will. Truth served men, not God.

Speaking for the purity of the mind and its activities, i.e., speaking for a form of thinking which he loved, Valéry said that "whatever our mind wants, the origins it seeks, the results and solutions it thirsts after, all these it cannot help deriving from itself, suffering them in itself. Cut off from experience, isolated from the constraints imposed by direct contact, the mind engenders what it needs, in its own fashion" ("A Fond Note on Myth," 55). How easily we criticize such a view of the mind, how many arguments we build up against it! How delightfully intelligent we feel when we launch our criticisms against Valéry and come forth like David, cheered by the crowd. In the solitude of our thought we discover something else. We find the autonomy of mind deeply struggling to be free of objects and ideas, but never truly free. Valéry has held up before us the wonders of the mind and has done it with a nobility and marvel that have rarely been equaled. The question is never that of its truth or falsity, but of its ideality. With the sense of political reality that Valéry developed in the mid thirties, he joined this sense of ideality, a sense he never lost even though many of his commentators see in such works as *Mon Faust* a deeper appreciation of the senses, in particular of the sense of touch. It would be difficult to find the stress on the senses a weakening of the rational and reasonable. Valéry was always loyal to Descartes. He represented, in the midst of a Europe that had moved toward madness, a tradition that had fewer and fewer believers in critical rationality, of the productive imagination and that deep sense of limitation. These were his guidelines. In them he developed his politics, the fine expression of a reasoned rationalism and universalism in post-World War I Europe. In speaking of the mind, I find Valéry witty, delightful, and often jolly. He said, speaking of the mind, "a mistake, a misunderstanding, a pun can fertilize it. It gives the name of science and art to its power of conferring upon its own phantasmagoria, a clarity, a duration, a consistency, and even a rigor astonishing to itself – sometimes even overwhelming!" ("A Fond Note on Myth," 45).

I take great pleasure reading these words. I know they are valid because I have experienced them. I know that myth no longer weeps. The future, it is sure, will bring us hope. The evil forces will be tamed, although never extinguished. They will bring havoc where they can, but our knowledge of them will limit their carnage. These are hopes and their reality is like the wanderer in the desert with the vast lands of sand before him and no oasis in sight. He believes there is one. He goes forward. If we speak of a Valéryean politics, then we say that its guide and objective is the enhancement of the human mind. We have learned to bet on it.

* * * *

Valéry spoke about women's rights in an article entitled "The Intellectual Destiny of Woman" (1928). I mention this article and others associated with it because they reflect his interest in social problems and his ability to speak of them intelligently. He was always well-informed. His concern for social issues reveals his never-ending request for understanding. The more we discover the depths of Valéry's thought, the more we are overwhelmed by his social and political concerns. If I didn't know that he was a poet, a playwright, a literary critic and theorist, I could be convinced that he was a master of political affairs. Listen to the manner by which he ended his article on "The Intellectual Destiny of Woman." He said: "It is not impossible that the domain of the arts may one day fall completely under the power of women, and that personalities may appear in music and philosophy as great as

Semiramus or Catherine in politics" ("The Intellectual Destiny of Woman," in *History and Politics*, 285). This is a heroic sentence. It has found its justification in contemporary politics in the U.S., England, and France. Valéry could smile if he wished.

Valéry had a subtle sense of humor and his addresses to audiences brought this forth with distinction. On November 28, 1931, he gave an introductory talk at a forum on "Woman" at the Université des Annales. His lecture was called "O Femme, qui donc es tu?" a delightful title. Valéry gave many lectures at the Université des Annales. He appeared at least twenty-one times and gave fifteen lectures (1927-39) (note to p. 290 in *History and Politics*, 594). Apart from these details, perhaps another should be added: These lectures began in 1907 and ended in 1940.

Valéry opened the conference on women with these words: "Ladies, and even Gentlemen, you are about to hear two voices [the one voice was that of Helen Vacaresco, and the other, La Duchesse de la Rochefoucaud], not discordant but harmoniously attuned, though successive and contrasting. They will talk to you about what might be called, 'The Intellectual Destiny of Women.' I am here only to furnish the prologue, as it were, to their eloquence" ("The Passion for Intelligence," in *History and Politics*, 286). There is a delicate and conscious art of conviction and persuasion in Valéry's addresses. He knows the vital importance of the audiences, and he embraces them with concern and ease. He wants them to listen willingly to what he has to say. Personality and word are inseparable. The rhetorical thinker knows this well. He cultivates relationship with facial expressions and appearance. Nothing is more vital to the statesman than the ability to handle an audience intelligently. Avoiding the problems of feminism, the total absorption of the women into political and military life, Valéry swings in the air, as Aristophanes imagined Socrates doing, and joins the woman problem to that of the intellect. "We are thinking," Valéry remarked, "of the place woman may aspire to fill, not in the State, not in the political system and the councils of government, but in the world of the Mind, I mean in the great enterprise of increasing our capital of knowledge and of beautiful things, a capital which humanity...builds and hands on from century to century" ("The Passion for Intelligence," 287). These are observations we would like to pass over in silence. We think of the places women must fill in government, in opposition to governments, in the struggle against injustice and for equality. Wherever there are struggles for the freedom of the mind in both domestic and foreign affairs, women struggle side by side with men. No! They do not belong only to a republic of the mind. This weakens them and reduces them to the illusions of men demanding the right to place women wherever they will. The differences which

Valéry makes between Eve's choice and Adam's leave us bewildered. We turn away pleased to pass on to another nuance of the subject.

Valéry reminded the ladies, "And you, young ladies, are too well educated to be unaware, that until the year 835 of the Christian era you had no soul, for certain. Some of the Church Fathers held you to be charming animals. Not until 835 did the Council of Agde or elsewhere, after long, subtle, and rigorous dispute, officially recognize that women have souls. This was not a very honorable condition, but it was not without its advantages. The Council, dear ladies, is perhaps mythical" ("The Passion for Intelligence," 290). There is a charm in all this, a mixture of pleasantries and delights. The issues are serious. They are to be handled with care and goodwill. Valéry and we are both pleased and saddened by what he says. We are living six decades beyond his remarks, living in countries other than France, having experienced women's rights movements successfully and unsuccessfully fought. The enfranchisement of women is now a theoretically acceptable fact. We find delightful Valéry's descriptions. His charm was his truth. "I remember," Valéry noted, "in my childhood, ladies seemed to me enormous and marvelous insects, or humans of operetta, or heroes of adventure and combat – but of what combat I had as yet no idea....They were also tyrants who obliged little boys to be polite, and in whose presence even men had to talk as they didn't talk among themselves. All this is greatly changed" ("The Passion for Intelligence," 291). I could imagine hearing this talk and appreciating it dearly. The content is of lesser importance than the delivery. The wording was a literary wonder. All is organized and prepared. We walk away knowing that we are listening to a master who is charming us about a serious problem. How enticing were his letters in that Republic of Letters to which he became devoted and powerfully commanding. In him Europe, and he hoped Asia, had found its intellectual leader.

What we admire deeply in Valéry is his opening to the future. In this world of fable and changing circumstances and possibilities lies the unexpected and unknown. It is the dream that haunts us, that has awakened the imagination, that hastens our excitement. The present is the starting point of our actions, the past remains the unknown element of the fable, the future the awakening of our beliefs and hopes. Valéry asked: "What will that new woman be like? And what will be her place in the life of man when the political distance, the difference in culture and occupation between the two sexes has more or less disappeared?" ("The Passion for Intelligence," 292). The answers to these questions will always be forthcoming. Every decade will make its own evaluation from its own experience. The answers of one age will be conjectures for another. Answers dissolve into conjectures. In this way they become meaningful answers. The politics of social life requires more than voting yes or no on social issues, of learning how to support one side and reject the other.

Ending his lecture "Le Suffrage des femmes," published in the *Revue de Paris,* February 15, 1931, Valéry astutely remarked: "I do not like the new because it is new, nor the old because it is old. I consider it neither difficult nor interesting to want to create an artificial future simply by reversing the present or to want *what has been* to outline its reasons for having been. The difficult thing is to link memory with fact... to understand what will be irresistible, and to give it, by foresight and intelligence the aspect of a desirable change wisely achieved" ("Woman Suffrage," in *History and Politics*, 300).

We observe with care Valéry's choice of expressions. I find a sense of *phronesis* in many of his remarks. What am I referring to with that Greek word? I would say that *phronesis* is practical wisdom separated from theoretical wisdom. Together with this wonderful word, Aristotle speaks of *sophrosyne,* a sense of measure, the avoidance of extremes. I have no desire to reduce Valéry to the Aristotelian gentleman or statesman. In these two words lies the sense of measure and harmony that characterizes Valéry's social and political attitudes. Listen again to a few of his words in a lecture he gave on February 3, 1934, on "The Question of Universal Suffrage." He said: "It is agreed, ladies, that, in equity and reason, you have every right to take part in political action. But there are those who fear the unknown that would follow from your casting a vote, who are afraid that some very convenient arrangements would be disturbed, some well established local or parliamentary positions upset" ("The Question of Universal Suffrage," in *History and Politics*, 304).

These are words that seek balance. They protect the future and its possibilities and at the same time, they guard the present, avoiding ideological and revolutionary expressions. Valéry is amusing when he needs to be. I would imagine that his listeners were delighted with his tonalities. Speaking of law in a previous lecture, he said: "It institutes and protects marriage but immediately informs us that woman thereby becomes a minor. In marriage a minor, in free love an adult!" ("Woman Suffrage," 299).

I have always been convinced that politics is a work of art. As we pursue this art with Valéry, we discover the truth which lies in a commentary he made to his work on Leonardo da Vinci. It is a short, but profound, morsel. Valéry states that "a work of art should always teach us that we had not seen what we see." This pungent remark points to the art of the statesman who is always beyond what he sees, and deeper than what he hears. As we begin this journey with him, we are prepared to follow him into the far corners of the mind, into the intricacies of morality. We recognize in Valéry a universality often expressed but hardly realized. In the decade of the thirties, Valéry emerged as *the* intellectual of Europe. He was the only David on the horizon. There was betrayal, cowardice, and fear. These demons would be more powerful than any David.

4

The League of Nations

I read a contemporary author called Jorge Semprun. The book was called *Literature or Life*. I felt attached to the book. I suddenly came across a remark that startled me, and I know why. I believe that it is necessary to explain one's reaction. Semprun was discussing the impact of Heidegger's *Sein und Zeit*, and the questions that arose from this book and his reactions to them. He observed that he believed "the fundamental inquiry underlying Heidegger's was quite simply unimportant. The question of why is there Being rather than nothing, has always seemed meaningless to me. It is not only bereft of meaning, but bereft as well of all possibility of producing any" (*Literature or Life* [New York: Viking, 1997], 93). I thought of this observation by Semprun because it attaches itself to my work on Valéry. Valéry is important not because of his interpreters, but because he is Valéry. This answer to my doubts clears the path for study, thinking, and writing. The question is not whether the choice is literature or life, but a life that creates literature and a literature that not only makes life more visible, but also searches for it in the invisible. The question leads to another less theoretical and more substantial one. World War I had made deep caverns in the European mind. Countries were arranged and rearranged. They were left weakened and strengthened. Too many men had died, too much talent lost, but this was no cure for national and international ambitions. There was a League of Nations, a visible body established to maintain peace. Europe was tired. Tiredness brings forth magnificent words and breaths of hope. There was a tired hopefulness. In 1926, Valéry proposed "An Exchange for Literary Values." In 1922, the League of Nations had created the Committee on Intellectual Cooperation. From this committee arose a subcommittee. Valéry was a member. He published his proposal in *L'Europe nouvelle*, January 16, 1926. He called his piece "Il faut créer une bourse des valeurs littéraires," (An Exchange for Literary Values).

Valéry began his text with remarks that affect every writer. We must take seriously the efforts to make the cultures of nations known to others. In fact, we build bridges through translations. The translation is the creation of a new text. It is the old text in new and different form. It is communicable. It communicates indifferently. People need to be known to each other. In one way or another, bridges are possible. Translations are the work of the imagination. There may be no bridge for a particular poem. The fact is that no one has found the way to allow a work in one language to pass immediately into another. We must trust the readers to find ways in their reading to grasp the meaning or images that are given to them. Translations don't end, they cause other translations.

The history of the text begins. Every great text has its history, and the history of its translations. Every great musical score belongs to its conductors, orchestras, and soloists. Valéry mentioned the works of Poe and Baudelaire. He remarked that Baudelaire's translations and praise made them famous throughout the world, not excepting the country of their origin" ("An Exchange for Literary Values," in *Politics and History*, 536). Without weighing the good and the bad of translation, we think of the powers of communication, the powers of knowledge and poetry. Valéry believed that the committee must do everything possible to encourage translations, award prizes, establish journals. Valéry believed deeply in the capacities and abilities of the mind. He was its champion.

In 1931, the subcommittee became the Permanent Committee on Arts and Letters. We list some of its members: Béla Bartok (Hungary); Karel Copek (Czechoslovakia); Henri Focillon (France); Julian Luchaire (France); John Masefield (England); Salvador de Madariaga (Spain); Thomas Mann (Germany); Gheorghe Oprescu (Romania); Helène Vacaresco (Romania); Paul Valéry (France); Josef Strzygowski (Austria); Ugo Ojetti (Italy); Roberto Paribeni (Italy); Ragnar Ostberg (Sweden).[*] We read familiar and unfamiliar names. We are struck by the eminence of the committee. For the moment we forget the cruder forces at work. We must forget them if we are to believe that rationality is the essence of man.

The members were to meet in different cities every year. In 1932, the first session was held at Frankfurt am Main, in commemoration of the centenary of Goethe's death. Valéry's talk was a shortened version of an address given at the Sorbonne on April 30, 1932, entitled "Address in Honor of Goethe." In Frankfurt his talk was called "Comment je vois Goethe." The following year in Madrid, Valéry spoke of "The Future of Culture." It is not our purpose to study the events at each session, but to discover Valéry's ceaseless attempt to find the meaning of the European

---

[*] This material is available in Appendix 3 of *History and Politics*, 531-34.

mind, to become acquainted with its nuances, the details of its functioning, and its ability to clarify ideas and dreams. More and more, I believe, it was at these conferences that Valéry achieved the pinnacle of his statesmanship, a commanding stature that brought respect and honor to his leadership and convictions.

We search for something that facts will not give us. We search for a quality, a particular and peculiar characteristic that distinguishes one man from others. I am not seeking for Valéry the poet, or playwright, or literary theorist. I am concerned with the statesman, the man who speaks for European civilization, whose voice is recognized throughout the civilized world, in every one of its cultural expressions. The only measure we have are his writings dedicated to this theme, but I wonder if more than the voice is needed. I believe that the content of his remarks celebrates the essence of this civilization. It celebrates what each European can hold on to and carry with him. This is essential. The capacity for recognition is that of creativity. In it lies Valéry's greatness. We can hold on to his words. We repeat them with pleasure and satisfaction. We trust them, and are loyal to them. We constantly learn from them. Let us for the moment turn to Valéry's words pronounced in 1933 in Madrid. Before he gave the final remarks, he paid respect to Miguel de Unamuno, saying: "I see before me in this meeting two great physicists, an eminent doctor, one of the most distinguished biologists, and a mathematician of the rank of M. Severi. I see also what I shall call an Unamuno – I shall not try to define him; he is a special category in himself, a unit that will not break down into multiples" (notes to "The Future of Culture," in *History and Politics*, 609-10). A distinct charm in Valéry's expressions came forth when he recognized others in the spirit of friendship created in these conferences.

The struggle against totalitarianism had begun. In 1932, Japan occupied Manchuria and the Manchukuo Republic was proclaimed. In January 1933, Hitler is declared chancellor. The events were bubbling. The volcano was about to erupt. An uneasiness swept Europe. The bubbling lava waited for its release.

Valéry spoke in an unhappy land. There were anarchist revolts in Barcelona whose consequences would tear Spain apart in civil war. Valéry remarked: "Although I am in Spain, and although I see Señor de Unamuno here, you have before you an assemblage of Don Quixotes – Don Quixotes of the mind, fighting their windmills....In particular, one of the aspects of the present Spanish experiment that strikes us, and must especially do so, is the fact that you have summoned intellectuals to the highest posts in the state. Spain has ministers and ambassadors, some of them present here, who are our intellectual brothers" ("The Future of Culture," 537). With subtlety, Valéry had begun to form the weapon that would be given to every honest intellectual for this coming battle against the irrationalism of the dictators, against a morality which served personal and national interests. This weapon was the purity of the mind, its freedom of development and creativity. This was the weapon. We needed not only to possess it, but to use it well. Valéry was the model. He was the leader, the one who drew respect from the others, who would cause them to see that the sanctity of the mind would preserve it from multiple attacks. We must realize that the study of ideas is impossible from political events. Japan had announced its departure from the league, a painful and threatening omen of what was to come. The Second World War was beginning. It began at the end of World War I. With Hitler's assumption of power, a national campaign of anti-Semitism commenced. We listen to Valéry's remarks, but we must not forget the events which were beginning to take shape. He knew these well. He followed politics in detail. The crisis was stated. He found it in his mind.

Valéry spoke of *a policy for the mind.* It was extremely difficult to discover a thought, an expression, that would unite not only Europe but Asia. The foundation of every civilization and culture is created in the mind, in art, in architecture, and science. We don't know why a civilization goes in one direction and then in another. We wonder about the inventions that come forth in Asia and not in Europe, or in Europe and not in Asia. In these lie the multiplicity of the universality of the mind. It unites humankind. We long to discover, in whatever part of the world we are at, how things are made and thought about. What drives humans to do something in one way and not in another, to hold certain beliefs, and ignore others? The sacred element is always the mind, the sacred process is its operations. Where these are threatened, the mind is threatened. Even if humans are not conscious of what is happening, the happening itself must be comprehended. If men and women are serious about the human endeavor, then they must be concerned with every attempt to discover the powers of human awareness, and the processes by which things are created. It is for this reason that Valéry remained close to the developments of science, to the thinking of Einstein and Freud. He was profoundly convinced that great minds should correspond. He thought of conversations and correspondence, debates and letters. He believed that the results should be published in two series of volumes under the auspices of the International Institute of Intellectual Cooperation in Paris.

At the end of the address in Madrid, Valéry said: "All politics imply an idea of man and of man's duty. Working out these ideas is an essential task. It is therefore natural to think that those who are dedicated to clarifying, criticizing, and formulating ideas as such must not be ignored by the public authorities and deprived of all but the scattered, unorganized, and indirect results of their writings and influence" ("The Future of Culture," 539-40). Sixty years later, we say the same thing, but with lethargy. The intellectuals have discovered that their bite is far weaker than their thought.

Together with Henri Focillon, Valéry wrote an introduction to the volume *Correspondance I: Pour une société des ésprits,* published in French and English by the Institut International de Co-opération Intellectuelle, Paris, in 1933 (note to "Toward a Correspondence," in *History and Politics,* 599). The opening words are significant. I realize now what is true in Valéry's opening statement. They jointly agreed upon the beginning words. The beginning sentence stated clearly the aim and purpose of Valéry's activities which he shared with the great art historian Henri Focillon. The opening remarks reinterpreted the theme which grew in significance with every passing year. Valéry grew more and more convinced that the human mind was the expression of man's uniqueness, that collectively it defined a civilization, and in smaller groups created a culture. A precious and sacred reality gave birth to Europe. The introductory remarks began with these words: "By inviting men of thought to consult together and exchange their views on the great problems of the life of the mind, on the present and future intellectual activity, the League of Nations is pursuing one of its essential aims....The League of Nations hopes to group around itself those men most capable of enlightening world consciousness and each other, at a particularly crucial moment in the life of the world....The League of Nations presupposes a league of minds" ("Toward a Correspondence," 349). We wonder what it means to become more and more immersed in the politics of the time. In 1918, Lenin, Trotsky, and Stalin came to power. Mussolini had in 1922 marched on Rome, and formed a Fascist government. Europe was breeding vipers. They came forth quickly and numerously. The intellectuals were organizing committees. We watch the committees take on, in words alone, the Communists, the Fascists and now the Nazis. In 1936, Francesco Franco takes over Spain; Japan takes Manchuria; Mussolini, Abyssinia. The generals are happy to have Franco. Now they are dictators. Franco advocates a policy of nonintervention, a safe and prosperous policy.

We go back to Spain in 1933 and to a speech that Valéry gave. We go back to men who believed that the struggle for reason was the supreme struggle of a civilization. We have believed that technological educations make a man or a woman capable of envisioning the needs of the intellect. We deeply betrayed reason. We still have our dictators and our civil wars with their monstrous atrocities. We have a deeper betrayal of reason than has ever been possible. We have equaled the technological and scientific education with one that is devoted to values belonging exclusively to the mind. We remember Socrates' words at the end of the "Apology," telling us that where he can no longer question his fellowmen, their life no longer exists for him.

Valéry noted that "the history of civilization, as well as the life of people, is made up not only of public acts and literary monuments, but of an enormous number of mute dialogues and wordless conversations between those who think. Superimposed on this network of relations is another – interchanges of conscious, accidental or arranged encounters, colloquies, and exchanges of correspondence" ("Toward a Correspondence," 349). It is fascinating to think that civilization is being built by these conversations and these correspondences taking place everywhere in the world. We think of shared techniques and disciplines, cooperative enterprises revealing an amazing diversity of research, communication, and shared methods. We see language barriers collapse, cultural patterns yielding enough to make social and economic relationships not only feasible but also natural. It seems as if the surface shows amazing exchanges of ideas, business agreements, and mutual support, the undersurface guards the cultural tradition, particularly languages and customs. Interdependence preserves at the same time profound dependence. We think horizontally and vertically. Thought goes in more directions than we can imagine. It weaves together the threads of a culture, but these can be woven into so many patterns that we fear that no particular pattern will ever dominate the others. We must be aware that one dictator, one party, one ideology pulls the threads apart, burns them in fires, and celebrates its activity with the dances of Bacchus. This haunts us. In fact, it terrorizes us. How is it possible to face the power of the dictator? Are we deceiving ourselves when we put our faith in intellectuals who speak, correspond, and deeply believe in what they say? Why, we shudder to say, are the forces of thought so hopelessly weak when they encounter the forces of evil? The texts we cite are powerful in their directness and insight. They are truthful. They are important. Valéry's remark is startlingly realistic, ideal and joyful. "The notion of a 'republic of letters' does not apply to a professional group, but to men variously imbued with an equal sense of the great urgencies of the mind, devoted in their very essence, to intellectual activity, and organized to insure its efficacy" ("Toward a Correspondence," 350).

Valéry and Focillon dreamed of this new "Republic of Letters" and the "League of Minds." These are dreams which each of us must have. There is no way of living a life which is identified with existential reality. Belief has a peculiar and unique strength. It faces its enemy, knows that the will must not be destroyed. It yields nothing. Belief is a stubborn phenomenon, unconquerable before the most horrifying events. We believe, even if that belief is madness and mockery. Is it possible to believe in rationality, knowing that irrationality has powers great enough to destroy it? Rationality is our dream. It was crushed and arose from its ashes. Aid came to these ashes from many places. Rationality was created with the soul. It was before the creation and will be after it. It is present wherever the mind is conscious of itself, where it longs for freedom and where its strength is rooted in hope and conviction. Valéry remarked that the League of Nations has many committees, but it has decided in the creation of the League of Minds and the new Republic of Letters to deal with individual human beings, to bind them to each other through letters. We are still working from individual to individual. We wonder if the mind can ever free itself from fatal conditions. This is its strength and its weakness. This leads us to a mystery we have not yet solved. We are tortured by a paradox that reveals both debility and strength, a strength fated by the gods, a weakness decreed by them. Valéry announced the first problem that should confront us: "In the present state of the world what is, and what should be the role of the intellect? Every modern activity, in particular politics and economics is governed and dominated by *myth* in the forms of ideologies" ("Toward a Correspondence," 352). It is these myths that terrify us. Rationality doesn't penetrate wise protective walls. It admits failure. It moves away with gentleness and dignity. Often its dignity is gone. What is left is the simple will to live, to survive. After Hitler came to power, intellectuals signed up in vast numbers to preserve their jobs. They claimed to be loyal to the party. What stunning pictures it made. Teachers and professors were seeking to preserve their jobs. They shut down their moral sense. They pretended that it didn't exist. They were convinced – they believed that they were convinced – that they were believers in the myth of impure Jews , and their ally, the Capitalist. Racial superiority is very attractive. Why not be a believer? The lie became overwhelmingly powerful. It is delightful to watch it work. This is what we do eagerly. For some inexplicable reason, we believe that rationality is the principle of civilization. A harmless belief, wounding no one. It convinces no one. We must believe. All cannot be given to skepticism. Are not belief and skepticism the political weapons?

We mentioned Salvador de Madariaga's letter to Valéry. We said that we would return to the letter written by Valéry to Salvador de Madariaga. Valéry wrote to Salvador de Madariaga in 1933. It was published in *Correspondance I: Pour une société des esprits*. This letter is a reply to de Madariaga's letter of the same year. Valéry spoke of belief and confidence. He knew that without these elements no opposition to totalitarianism is possible. The crowds learn to believe quickly. They need charismatic leaders with shiny boots, like Hitler. The intellectual believes slowly. His mind weighs the options. He is stymied by the multitudes of possibilities. He becomes confused. Too many conditions come forth. He is weakened. He becomes quiet. He is immobile. The intellectual is clever and cunning, but profoundly inept. He avoids confrontation. He is a tired being.

Valéry began his letter with these significant words: "If we were more intelligent and gave the mind more place and real power in the things of this world, this world would have a better chance to right itself, and that more quickly" ("Toward a League of Minds," in *History and Politics*, 355). We reach the word *PERHAPS*. This is the word of our despair which lies deeply in a soul that has witnessed the mortality of civilizations, whose optimism flows into pessimism. The soul that reads too much becomes hellish, weighed down with seagrasses becoming heavier and heavier. History bears down upon us like fate, forever to be a burden on us. We are terrified by what history shows us. We turn away from the shouting. It is only a fable. This is true, but the fable may be painful. It tells us about our nature. The Grimm brothers wrote shockingly vivid tales of human ugliness, murder, and horror. We must forget history. We must not retell its stories. We bring them too close to the divinities. We make them sacred. In closeness they become godlike. They entice us to believe. In their enticement, in their parodies and speeches, we move toward belief. We are swept up in the rages of evil, the marches which fill the cities and the rhetoric, but most of all, by the new arts of communication. We watch the films of Leni Riefenstahl and see the fantastic displays of organized human action. I refer in particular to her *Triumph of the Will* released in 1935/36. Will the word have a chance of righting itself? We must believe that it will. There must be a "will to believe." William James caught the precise words. We are driven into exile by our nature to create, to be dissatisfied. Sadly, we reflect upon our opponents, upon a world filled with civil wars ending in killing fields.

Valéry described well what it looks like, the world of national states seeking domination and status. He stated: "It seemed that nothing could hold, nothing could last and keep its identity, caught up in that excited energy, where at every moment in a whirl of *dissociations* we could see the elements and systems of the old world, the contradictory principles and opposed activities uniting and dividing, combining and falling apart. The change from *dream to reality* and from *reality to dream* was, so to speak, furiously accelerated" ("Toward a League of Minds," 356).

We relate a story of tensions and resentments, of hatreds and errors. We relate the history of humankind. We relate the tale of a man who fought against it. In fact, we don't relate a true story. There are the wonders of mind and will in every period of human history. Each tells its own story and supplies myriads of detail. We wonder which is our story. Where do we belong? We know that we belong here and not there. We are children of space and time although our creation often surpasses both space and time. Everything seems to be mixed. We yearn to belong to the timeless, to join that limited group of tireless beings whose works have placed them in a unique paradise. We love the experience of time and place. Here we enjoy the urges of our nature, the senses which give us such great pleasure. We are children of many worlds, never knowing to which we belong fully. Happily we belong to none. Valéry asked: "What an age is this, when the serpents of the world are all swallowing their own tails!...Is there now anything on earth – any way of life, thought, or work, any leisure, any situation – that is not at the mercy of some discovery, invention, telegram, reflex, or vote?" ("Toward a League of Minds," 356). We are fascinated by these changes and desire more and more of them. Happily changes take place at different movements in various fields of endeavor. We cry out for bits of sanity, for a place on the moon with slumbering scholars. Ubu, whose mother was Cassandra, headed our community. I invented such a place but I tired of the isolation, I wanted to be closer to the earthly confusion. It had its own excitement which I found good for my sense of balance. I needed to look closely at my fellowmen. I needed to watch them indiscriminately. I needed to see starved and sick children. No man or woman has the right to be sheltered from these events. He needs the muck. It enlightens his soul. Horrors are good for the soul. It makes it yearn for order and quietude, often for the dictator.

On November 12, 1933, 92 percent of the voters in Germany elected Nazi candidates. The fates had decided. The future is terrifying. We hid from this terror. We had exhausted all the corners and all the burrows. We ran to the lie and hid in its wrinkles. There was no other place to go. There was no PERHAPS. We were sure. A madman had entered German power. How could it be? Civilization returned to barbarism. It seemed to fade away. We smile with despair. We know that we don't know. In this ambiance of not knowing, we find the limits of knowledge, the significance of the senses. In this turmoil, we seek for rational resolutions. Man's judgment is fallible, often more fallible than we dare admit. I give you a well-known example: Léon Blum's evaluation of the Nazis coming to power. Blum was an intelligent and honorable man. Listen to him for the moment: "Hitler," wrote the editor of *Populaire* in *Les Problèmes de la paix* (1931), "is further from power today than General Boulanger in the evening of the 27th of January 1889....Ought we fear that he will approach it? According to me, No. I believe that Hitler's star has already reached its high point, its zenith. I believe it for reasons that I have for a long time enunciated....When once installed in the

Chancellery, this absurd buffoon of racism would suddenly feel on his shoulders the heavy weight of prudence, and circumspection. His program would become embarrassing, both for Germany itself, and for the outside world. We have seen many of these opportunistic metamorphoses.

"...Neither Germany's military power nor its prestige is such that it could group under its sway half of Europe. This it did fourteen years ago" (Jean Lacouture, *Léon Blum* [Paris: Editions du Seuil, 1977], 251). We read this evaluation. We smile. We feel terribly fallible, weak, and inadequate. Political thinking in its immediate circumstances is delightfully intelligent or foolish, clever, inadequate, and cunning. It is blind, foolish, and amazingly inept. What are the guideposts? However learned we are in national histories, in international relations, in political biographies, there is that Aristotelian virtue of prudence, that sense of balancing right and wrong which seems to have been given to few of us. It is a natural ability, a gift of nature, an endowment.

Valéry observed that "the gap is immense between on the one hand our habits, our institutions, our legislation, even our sensibility, and on the other, what we know and are capable of knowing, what we will and are capable of willing" ("Toward a League of Minds," 357). How do we act and think in a field dominated by chance and contingency? Possibility succumbs to possibility and yet there is the need for decision, for a political direction, for a moral position which allows other nations to judge the quality of our commitment. Again Valéry balances one form against another. "On the one hand," he said, "technique, preparation, accuracy, control, order, and precision; on the other, expedience, verbal trickery, illusions, various superstitions of a philosophical or historical kind, party prophecies, naive symbols playing upon impulse or innuendo" ("Toward a League of Minds," 377). Who would want to be in such a realm? The Greeks honored the statesman, gave him all the honors which a society could give to an individual. They found words to explain the qualities which set the statesman apart from other men, which caused us to believe that he is the possessor of capacities which can't be shared. These men knew how to organize disorder, to bring strength and hope to those filled with despair and indifference. The ruler created a spirit, a loyalty that is beyond normal adherence. He uses technology to impart truth, to make it seem as if the changes in society are necessitated naturally, guided by scientific certainties. Strategy has become scientific, even to the deployment of troops and heavy equipment. War is scientific. Peace follows fixed and absolute demands. This is a peace that ends in war. We struggle against contingencies. We are bitterly opposed to myth, but everything has become myth.

"I confess," Valéry said, "the spectacle of the world of politics make me sick. I was doubtlessly not meant to contemplate it....The newspapers and radio bring the street and its events, with all their clamor and incoherence, right into our rooms" ("Toward a League of Minds," 359). Valéry spoke of a vulgarization, "a revolt of the masses" that had now begun to develop into a political power. Vulgarity was no longer limited to a psychological and sociological event. Vulgarity had become political. We addressed the vulgar. We spoke of them as a political power. We reminded them of 1792, the beheading of Louis XVI, of the good they have done for the body politic. We learned the importance of the vote and propaganda. Vulgarity is false equality. Vulgarity is the denial of morality. Power creates its right to act, to persecute, and to prosecute.

Valéry made it very clear that he regarded "the political necessity of exploiting all that is lowest in man's psyche as the greatest danger of the present time" ("Toward a League of Minds," 360). Valéry's pessimism was in defiance of his optimism. He spoke often of the decline of civilization, of its decrepitude and distortion. What is dominant in this thinking is the political accuracy of Valéry's thinking. He didn't foresee what was going to occur. He foresaw the moral and intellectual conditions. No, he was not a prophet. He never spoke of specific events to come. He spoke of tendencies, of attitudes, moods, and feelings. He understood deeply his own remark that civilizations are mortal, that progress was a myth, that retrogression was also a myth. What is ever present are the qualities of the gentleman. He was a gentleman. For each event and feeling there is a proper vocabulary, a proper means of execution, a strength and courage which lead the community rather than being led by it. The myth of man's indomitable ingenuity became an article of faith.

In speaking of hostilities between nations, Valéry made a penetrating observation. He knew that people don't fight each other. Governments make war upon each other for what they think is in the national interest. "Hostilities between nations," Valéry believed, "depend necessarily on a very limited number of persons, for nations themselves are political notions or entities that can be clearly conceived only by men of sufficient culture and imagination to comprehend and symbolize groups of millions of human beings, often extremely unlike (if not antagonistic) in type and interest..." ("Toward a League of Minds," 360). The nations are the dreams of their leaders, of their history and their traditions. Nations are fictions, spiritual and physical entities whose definitions are determined by the fable and by time. Their origins are fixed in history, in battles, in victories and defeats, in charismatic leaders. As we read through these works of the 1930s, we find ourselves confronted with a political Valéry we believed was not possible. It was always possible. I make no comparisons between the before and the after, between the mature and immature. These are false opposites and yield nothing valid for the interpreter. We see clearly only when we are dealing with nuances. The shades and resonances are subtle, and often truly perceptible, but they reveal surprisingly clear insights in their shadows. They are clear and precise. If we read with care, seeking to discover attitudes previously not described, we see everything as continuity. Change is less clear, but there is change, radical and significant change. This young man who worked for the Havas News Agency for twenty-two years for Edouard Lebey, its director, knew political life very well. We recall that Macchiavelli evaluated ambassadorial reports in Florence from ambassadors from all parts of Europe. This training was fundamental for his political judgment. Sorrowfully, we regret that it has not been spoken of adequately. It is a fundamental training. It was Valéry's training with Edouard Lebey.

Valéry knew well that the transformation of the human world would make violence a necessity. Violence is the vehicle of radical change. This is clear, without the least appeal to sentimental considerations. So I came back to my beginning, which was an invocation to the intelligence of men. I repeat Valéry's words: "More brain, O Lord." It is often stated that Valéry spoke little about morality, that the will was more developed than the intellect. This is not true. Valéry spoke of intellect with passion. This is a moral attitude. It was created in a moral commitment. Every attempt to weaken the mind, to suffocate and control it was wrong, fiercely perverse. This perversion forced us to sacrifice our lives. There is no life without the intellect. There is existence. He concluded a letter to Salvador de Madariaga with these words: "When I said one day at Geneva, at one of the meetings of our Committee that the League of Nations presupposed a League of Minds, I mean simply that no one understood it better than you" ("Toward a League of Minds," 361).

In the midst of what we call progress in every individual field, we find a lack of purpose. Why are these advances coming? Has man become more conscious of the moral problem? Does he think of his civilization? I know that there is a need to think. Man needs illusion, but rarely needs to think. We can do all that we need to do, without thinking. Thinking, however, makes it possible for us to do something in a particular field. It lifts the bonds of subjugation to the past in a way that shows us our freedom, the vastness of possibilities and the multitude of conjectures that are necessary for meaningful life. What are we studying when we come to politics? Valéry answered this question with this answer: "All politics, even the simplest, amounts to a speculation on man, a kind of reasoning and action applied to men and groups of men. The grounds for such action are fictitious, whereas its effects are real enough – only too real in some circumstances" ("Toward a League of Minds," 359).

On July 3, 1933, a pact was signed in Rome linking Britain, France, Germany, and Italy to the League Covenant, the Locarno treaties, and the Kellogg-Briand Pact. Skepticism would destroy our capacity to comprehend the hopes and dreams which joined nations in a community for peace and disarmament. Skepticism hides. It returns hope to the shadows. Humankind could not be more pleased. Nations signed a treaty. Do they really trust each other? There are sparks of optimism. Orators exploit the theme of peace. They say that even Hitler is not totally evil. Many wanted us to recognize his good side. We said nothing. Fair play forced us to plead for him. We are reasonable men and women. We yelled for all to hear: Give the man a chance. Chamberlain would repeat the call to the very end during the occupation of Czechoslovakia at the beginning of the invasion of Poland in 1939. We were deceived, but we were rational men. We were filled with delusions. We trusted human nature and from the center of Europe, Leni Reifenstahl told the story on film. A few of us knew. Simone Weil witnessed a dying Berlin, betrayal followed betrayal. They were pleased with our attitude. The Nazis conquered. Raymond Aron knew what was happening, but who would listen to him? Communism hid our faces from the specter of Nazism. Valéry was acting as a professor, informing us how we should approach the political and what we should be looking for. It sounded as if his speeches were still professorial lectures aimed at the ignorant for their welfare.

Valéry's descriptions were deeply insightful. They were called candid. Listen for a moment to a short paragraph he wrote in a preface to a book called *La Lutte pour la paix*. The year was 1933. Valéry wrote: "The most just and serious criticism which, in my opinion, can be leveled at the League of Nations is that it was not constituted, first of all, as a League. The League brings together individuals who represent an historical system of rivalry and discord. They bring to Geneva the best will in the world, but, along with it, a burden of mental reservations and the invincible habit of wanting to gain an advantage at someone else's expense" ("The Struggle for Peace," in *History and Politics*, 363).

We have often spoken of politics as a game of men and women who enjoy manipulating the nations of the world. Some rose to magnificent places of power. Some, like Lord Palmerston, Disraeli, Clemenceau, knew the game well, others like Gladstone played a moral game. The greater the statesmen, the greater the quirks; the finer the subtleties, the deeper the contradictions. Politics is often an outgrowth of history. We think of Woodrow Wilson. He knew too much. He thought too much. Medea had given him the professor's role and he had no idea of how to remove it. Valéry had no idea of becoming a professional statesman. He wanted to give voice to his belief in reason, to the formation of a community of men and women in search of intellectual communication. These were men of the mind, devoted to its purity, refusing to put it at the service of the state. I remember a remark he made in 1917 in a preface to the poems of André Lebey called "A Few Words." In it he remarked that "history finally leads to politics, just as Bacchus used to lead to Venus. History, in relation to politics, can act as an appetizer. It predisposes us, just as a menu can provoke a succulent foretaste of a dinner....Politics! At that word, I am overcome with silence. I am aware that I have nothing more to say!" ("A Few Words," in *History and Politics*, 518-19).

This silence is broken by events. From 1933 on, profound events would shake the foundations of European civilization. We recall that in 1936 Addis Ababa fell and Italy annexed Abyssinia. The cracks in the walls of Europe grew deeper and wider. The democracies grew weaker. Valéry called for a Republic of Minds. He believed in it. I would imagine that he had convinced himself of the necessity to believe. What else was left to him to believe?

Aesop has a delightful fable for us: "Zeus packed all the good things of life in a jar, put a lid on it, and left it in the care of certain men. Itching to know what was inside, the man lifted the lid. The contents immediately flew up into the air and departed from earth to heaven. Only Hope remained – for she was shut in when he clapped the lid on again. Mankind has only Hope to promise them recovery of the blessings they have lost" (*Fables of Aesop*, Penguin, 1974, no. 154).

5

Deeper into the Labyrinth of Politics

On January 6, 1935, at the Université des Annales, Valéry delivered a lecture called "The Outlook for Intelligence" (Le Bilan de l'intelligence), (1935). I don't believe that it is just another well-polished and thoughtful lecture created and formed by a poet and a superbly sophisticated prose writer. This lecture grasped the imagination of a serious public. I am not speaking of equally serious effects. Lectures don't have such effects. They are professional games and practices needed by every serious player. We discover in this lecture a stately symmetry of thoughts. They are set down as if one day they will be held up as an example of an ordered, harmonious, and beautifully structured introduction to thinking. Valéry was the master of such poetic prose. We are attracted also by the depths of ideas. We are forced to think, which may or may not be more pleasurable. This lecture was a work of art.

Valéry remarked that "the words 'sensational,' 'amazing' commonly used today, are the kind of words that describe an era. We can no longer bear anything that lasts. We no longer know how to make boredom bear fruit....We can no longer deduce from what we know a notion of the future to which we can give the slightest credence" ("The Outlook for Intelligence," in *History and Politics*, 130-31). A great joy has been taken from us. We are fascinated by the prophetic gift. We know that the false prophets are far more numerous than the true ones. Pretense to prophecy is a human skill, exercised exquisitely by those who learned the art. It is this insight into the ambiguous inflowing and outflowing of things that confuses us. Mortality is our fate. We feel as if we have been tied to time. There we learn resignation and surrender. We grow tired. "My helplessness," Valéry noted, "is a measure of the change that has taken place" ("The Outlook for Intelligence," 131). This is a helplessness that creates a strength. It surrenders but it arises from its own ashes. Helplessness in the present is strength in the past. In the present, we face the unknown, the conjecture, the possibilities. The past was formulated for our particular purposes, and is supposedly dominated by our thought. We are knowledgeable of the past. We tell a coherent story when referring to it. We are comfortable with the past. We make it fit our storytelling. Often, we tell wonderful tales and fables. Valéry remarked that "we no longer look upon the past as a son looks upon his father from whom he may learn something, but as a grown man looks on a child....At times we might even fancy reviving the greatest of our ancestors for the pleasure of instructing and astonishing them" ("The Outlook for Intelligence," 131). The generations no longer simply follow the generations. They look back and see the ancestors as primitives struggling to find solutions that the present has already, at least for the moment, found. We find it difficult to be without storytelling and we turn from people to people to discover their native stories. Often we are as fascinated by them. We become enamored with a new tradition. We begin to study it. We find delight in our discoveries. We feel that we have been captured by a new life that awakens in us new intellectual adventures. I think of the *Gitanjali* (1912) of Rabindranath Tagore, of my adventure into Indian spiritual life, of the works of Sri Aurobindo Ghose which have been with me throughout my life. I go back again and again to the *Gitanjali* of Tagore. It reads:

> Thou has made me endless, such is Thy pleasure. This
> frail vessel thou emptiest again and again, and fillest
> it ever with fresh life.
>
> This little flute of a reed thou hast carried over
> hills and dales and hast breathed through it melodies
> externally new. At the immortal touch of thy
> hands my little heart loses its limits in joy and
> gives birth to utterance ineffable.
>
> Thy infinite gifts come to me only on these very
> small hands of mine. Ages pass, and still thou
> pourest, and still there is room to fill.
>
> *(Gitanjali* [Song Offerings], London, 1919, 1).

We shifted away from the political but never for long. It seems as if we are dragged back to it by the fates, as Heraclitus believed. If the sun transgressed its path, the fates would put it back on course. There is no intellectual discussion where beauty has no place. There is no discussion that can't be inspired by beauty. The depths of the political soul lie in the hands of the muses. We cultivate politics. We seek to find our way to the leisure of the mind (*Scholé*). There are books that are important. They are read only for their beginning chapters. This is true for Aristotle's *Politics*. At the end Aristotle elaborated on the theme of leisure. He showed us how every art serves a purpose. About this purpose we make judgments.

"Music," he said, "serves none of these uses....We are thus left with its value for the cultivation of the mind in leisure. This is evidently the reason of its being introduced into education: it ranks as a part of the cultivation which men think proper to free men" (*Politics,* trans. Ernest Barber, Oxford, 1950, 8:8). If leisure is an activity and it is a very serious one, then it is at the service of the mind in judgment. I am often reminded that where there is no mental cultivation, the mind becomes instrumentality. With leisure, we cultivate the soul, the rationality which is our precious gift and our most formidable activity. Valéry knew Aristotle intuitively. He knew him by repetition.

There is little doubt that the statesman must cultivate the soul, must perceive man as the bearer of rationality. He must find in the nurturing of the soul the highest human activity. We seek to preserve a civilization because there is freedom in it. We value freedom. We value man. In the Europe of the 1930s, this evolution went through shocking changes. It showed the future with the Nuremberg laws, but this had already begun in different forms, but equally harsh, in Italy and the Soviet Union. Valéry had to do little but observe the events about him. Observation is never enough. We observe veils hiding realities which we can't approach, meanings that escape us or send us in obscure and purposeless directions. We pursue our work with pragmatic confidence. We have no other choices. These have been taken from us by the fates. We go forward with instinct, believing that what is precious to us is worth the battle, is worth death. The question of success or failure plays a limited role. There is no doubt that rationality and reason are indisputable forms of our existence. They are the essence of human life.

"In all human affairs," Valéry noted, "all the cards have been reshuffled. *Man is now assailed by questions that no man before had imagined,* whether philosopher, scientist, or layman; everyone has somehow been taken unawares. *Every man belongs to two eras*" ("The Outlook for Intelligence," 135). We have been taken unawares. The imagination couldn't grasp what had occurred. We are told that events took place before we recognized them, but there are events that no power of the imagination could grasp. We faced horrifying and monstrous events. Before, during, and after World War II, the poets, essayists, and novelists began to tell the story. Each told one that brought us to the nuances of the catastrophes.

The cards have been reshuffled, but we don't know exactly what this means. We see across the face of Europe the bubblings of changes that leave us distressed. We don't know what to say. Silence is often our answer. We call it nationalism, atavism, religious fundamentalism. In the midst of politics, we don't comprehend the emergence of an unimaginable technology and a highly sophisticated science, literature, and poetry. We put aside the veils. They are infinite. As one is drawn apart, another appears. This journey in the veils is characteristic of the journey we have decided to make. The journey seems purposeless. We don't know where we are going, in what port we will find provisions. The veils are large and lightly closed. We work hard to separate them. Our strength weakens. There are too many veils, heavy and defiant ones. Our energies weaken. We want to surrender to forces greater than ourselves. There is a futility in this never-ending battle. Surrender is hard. Rationality has been our existence, but its fullness has not been revealed. We struggled to enter the labyrinths of the rational. As we approach the veils get heavier and heavier. Our approach has made this possible, the heaviness of the veil is measured by our distance from the soul of rationality. Few humans see the face of reason. Again and again we are warned that man can't see the divine and rational face. The face of reason would destroy us. Its light would burn our eyes and dry our skin. We are resigned to the impenetrability of divine powers. These miraculous powers refuse to be identified with man and his efforts to dissolve into divinity. Mercifully, the divine pushes us away and leaves with a distance we will, and should, never overcome. We survive only because we don't overcome. We struggle fully for an ideal when we avoid identifying with it and we deny ourselves. It is this identification that is fraught with danger. The detail assumes to be the whole, to speak for the whole. It challenges all other details. Its voice is strident and prickly. Others run from it, but they have few places to go. They yield and fade into the whole.

Every man finds his preferences in either the question or the answer. The questioners find their satisfaction in interminable questioning. Others find only exhaustion and boredom. At a certain point their inquiry ceases. They yearn for answers. In power, the questioner abhors the question. They don't usually come. They come as temporary fill-ins. They are simple possibilities now defined as answers. "In the past," Valéry remarked, "the rare innovations that occurred were merely solutions or answers to problems or questions that were ancient if not immemorial. But our kind of innovation consists not in answers, but in the true novelty of the questions themselves, in the statement of problems, not in their solution" ("The Outlook for Intelligence," 136). The questions reflect the depth of our thinking. They no longer serve for identifications and the acquisition of information. They arouse the soul, they scatter our thoughts. The order crumbles as it is about to fall. We feel a metaphysical helplessness. The world has been taken from us. The answers don't easily come. We no longer trust commandments. They are lapidary. They attempt to cover more than is possible for them. We let them hang from the trees and use them as guideposts. The worthiness of our problems has been deeply questioned by the rising power of technology. What we do today would be madness for those who lived in the immediate past. Those who will live tomorrow will make us feel like primitives. What a profound metamorphosis!

We read Valéry's articles, his lectures, and we feel as if we are entering the realm of wisdom. We are being taught by a philosopher king giving us guidelines for behavior and for action. I think of Thucydides taking us through the Peloponnesian war, pointing out the weaknesses and strengths of men, showing their brilliance and their follies, their victories and defeats. The dialogue often dominated political negotiation and gave it reality and verve. The narrative which is evoked forces history to become human history. Valéry does the same through his essays, his reflections. At times, I feel as if I am approaching a wise man who cultivates wisdom literature. This is his way to communicate with his fellowmen. So much of what he says goes beyond dialogue, beyond confrontation. His remarks reflect a search for universality, for the Republic of the Mind. Speaking of the great worldwide activity of the mind, of the transformation of space and time into new images of movement and metamorphosis, Valéry mentioned that the "transformation of the human world has taken place in no order, on no pre-established plan, and above all, without regard to human nature – the slow pace of its adaptation and evolution, and its fundamental limitations" ("The Outlook for Intelligence," 137). The future appears to be shapeless. We turn to inexplicable events, to totalitarian leaders, to party hacks, and we wonder about the future. We listened to Winston Churchill. The greatest of French statesmen, L. Barthou, is assassinated in Marseilles. He knew well the totalitarian mind. The rages of thunder and lightning are everywhere. How do we arrange this picture? Every description fails to bring order. "It may be said," Valéry remarked, "that *everything we know*, which is to say, *everything we can do* has finally turned against what we are" ("The Outlook for Intelligence," 137).

We encountered wisdom. Our first emphasis is to remember it. Wisdom is not discussed. It goes into our thoughts. It becomes our thoughts. There, in mysterious ways, it is nurtured. It was always Valéry's manner to search for the clearness of truth, for the perfect description, the subtlety of expression, attempting to come closer and closer to the intellect. He was not a dialectician or a man of dialogue. He chose the way of the phenomenon. He bracketed it and observed how it merged, how it came forth from the mind. There was no object without consciousness. The mind created both subject and object. This that we call mind is man's holiest reality, not only in a religious sense, but from consciousness. Valéry was the thinker for whom consciousness was the highest moment of the human experience. It was natural for him to be the leader of those who sought to defend the European mind from any political party or government. In this intellectual leadership, Valéry emerged as the greatest defender of Europe's faith in reason. Even in those peripheral lands where reason's influence was slight, its leaders, at times, expressed their devotion to Aristotelian and Cartesian rationality. We know how deeply shaken Europe was after World War I, how quickly the age of progress gave way to skepticism, to Dada.

All sorts of pseudoexpressions illustrated the fantasies and monstrosities hidden in human existence. Man became madder than the descriptions of conventional madness. Valéry asked: "Can the mind get us out of the plight it has got us into?" ("The Outlook for Intelligence," 137). The question is fundamental. We speculate with fright about the survival of rationality. We are not speaking technical vocabularies. We speak of the rational vision of the world. We imagine the problem which accompanied the end of World War II. We feel as if we have buried the rational belief. It lay at the core of our civilization, the formative principle of our culture. Where do we go from here?

We seek clarification of what has occurred, of the worlds that have been lost and the worlds that are yet to be born. The answers swarm about us, each searching for a perch on which to land, a place from which it calls out its message. Many find their places. Many die of exposure and the lack of warmth. Many simply wither away. Valéry put it in an explosive form, one that casts doubt on what is happening. We wonder if we are capable of mastering the decisions we set in motion. The questions he raised were these: "Can the human mind master what the human mind has made? Can the human intellect save both the world and itself? My object then, is a kind of examination of the mind's current value and its future or probable value; that is the problem I have set for myself, and shall not solve" ("The Outlook for Intelligence," 138). The first question forges a dilemma we would like to avoid. We would like to believe that our creations can be mastered, but there is an amazing gap between creation and mastery. The gap is comprised of nuances swaying from the achievements of the human mind to the runaway accomplishments seeking their independence. They seek a wild freedom which becomes the source of resentment and mockery. We have always had art of madness which flourished with extraordinary powers. We wonder about the intellect and its meaning, its dominance and weakness. It seems to be a fleeting truth. It becomes an oddity when the imagination is nearby. We are concerned about its desertion, about the pale quantities of its expressions and forms. Science has seized it for its experimentations, and the technological advances which emerge from it. In the paleness of the intellect, we wonder about its survival. Its sickness seems to have no remedy. We group about it, proclaiming our faith in it.

We wonder what values these incantations have. There is little else we can do.

Is there no separation between existence and thinking? I am speaking here of the effect which life, political and social life, has upon individuals and nations. The loves and hatreds which emerge from religions, from the breakdown of multinational empires, become the shredded fabrics of people seeking to declare independence. Independence is the measure of a people's existence. It defines its culture and protects its language and literature. The great empires are gone. We watch the fledglings shape a national spirit, feeling equal to other peoples, competing with them happily. The sounds of the words are pleasant, the earth joins the sounds, songs of heroic paths lend themselves to the chorus. A symphony has arisen from the land, while in the blood acts of obedience justify the people before God. All has become myth.

Valéry, in a rare personal mood, told us about his hopes: "I hope to show the way in which modern life, the life of most men, affects their minds – influences, stimulates, or weaves them. I say that modern life affects the mind in such a way that we may reasonably feel great anxiety for the survival of intellectual values. The working conditions of the mind have, in fact, suffered the same fate as all other human affairs" ("The Outlook for Intelligence," 138). We wonder if any human event can be analyzed and classified, if we can grasp the extent of its implications and significance. Valéry turned toward the political world with a sense of balance and articulation. He brought to this world a wisdom that confronted the dictators, the civil wars, and the racial hatred. Perhaps he was, at times, unaware of the monstrosities that were appearing before him, but he was not naive. He could write: "I confess that I am so frightened by certain symptoms of degeneration and debility which I observe (or think I observe) in the general trend of intellectual production and consumption, that I sometimes despair of the future" ("The Outlook for Intelligence," 138-39).

There is an important advantage in rereading. The mind is awakened to what it ignored, to what it didn't realize. The implications of ideas are either diminished or enhanced. Rereading is a novel experience that can only be grasped by the reader when he has become a writer. Rereading gives us the past, the source of a knowledge we identify with history. We wonder if there is such a reality as history. We call it the fable, the narrative, the epic. We choose what we want to call history. We choose what we prefer. History is our game. We play it constantly. We clothe it in technological language. But history was a delightful story when left to the storyteller.

Valéry displayed a delightful seriousness when he dealt with the mind. He was honestly frightened when he thought of its weakening. He noted that "the mind might gradually succumb to the same indifference, inattention, and instability that many things in the present world, in its tastes, manners, and ambitions, either display already or give us cause to dread" ("The Outlook for Intelligence," 139).

In this uneasiness lies wisdom. There is no rushing to extremes to destroy the extremes. There is a prudence in Valéry that carries him from position to position. The denial is natural. There is an inner sense, a common sense, which defies ideologies and fanatic faith. Again we think of Aristotle, of *Nicomachian Ethics* and *Politics*. We think of the care demanded by the mind, the respect that we give to it. We wonder at the marvels it has given the world. We have not, to any extent, explored the powers of rationality. We watched its manifestation, its attempts to control its products. We have watched its failure and successes.

If we can't imagine a history of moral and intellectual progress, if events have destroyed this possibility, then we should mix moments of optimism with those of pessimism, ideals and utopias with disorder and chaos. But politics is more than a challenging of confronting forces. It is dominated by a goal and purpose which is not born in it but is imposed upon it by the philosopher, the sociologist, or the theologian. They are the masters of the art of story making. We get the history we make, the myths we need to hear. This making of history doesn't come forth arbitrarily. It is hinted at by the course of events. The hints and traces of meaning are ambiguous. The anxiety we feel in us disturbs the equilibrium between the good and the malicious, between the beautiful and the ugly. We ask with the intoxication of doubt about that vast realm of being lying between the one pole and the other. Mortality tolerates no vacuums. It wanders to mysterious places for ways to fill our history with purpose. For purpose we invent the gods, Egyptian gods, Hebraic gods, Greek gods, Hindu gods. We need them for all order. Valéry remarked that "there have been unstable species, monstrosities of size, power and unwieldiness that have not endured. Who knows if all our culture is not hypertrophy, a 'sport,' an untenable development, which a few centuries will have sufficed to bring into being and to an end" ("The Outlook for Intelligence," 139).

If we knew the origin of these things, our problems would fade away. We need our problems. They are the foods of our mind and body. Politics is very much more than a series of descriptions and definitions. We have never surpassed Aristotle's attempt to play biologist even with politics. There is, however, no bridge from biology to political thinking. The speculative elements in the political are essential. We must know less what a thing is than the values it has for us.

Men have thought of politics without values as if it were a self-moving and developing process. Politics is a natural phenomenon. This belief is hard to accept, although its plausibility is attractive. The most serious political theorist in our age was the German professor Carl Schmitt, whose notion of the confrontation between friend and foe is a serious attempt to make sense out of internal and international conflicts. More often than not, in the indescribable, we approach the truth. If we listen for a moment to a speech by Mussolini in October 1922 in Naples, we hear startlingly powerful words: "We have created a myth, this myth is a belief, a noble enthusiasm; it does not need to be reality, it is a striving and a hope, belief and courage. Our myth is the nation, the great nation which we want to make into a concrete reality for ourselves" (Carl Schmitt, *The Crisis of Parliamentary Democracy* [1923; reprint, Cambridge: Massachusetts Institute of Technology, 1985], 76). With this creation, Mussolini and other myth builders knew that they had destroyed parliamentary democracy. The myth is believed in. It is not debated. It crushes skepticism. It abhors doubt. Where myth dominates, discussion is put aside. Myth tolerates only the enhancement of the self and those institutions which are barriers to its development. Valéry gave myth great consideration, but he never identified it with the political state. He recognized it as the most devastating instrument of the political animal. The leader uses the myth well. It is a fine instrument in his hands. He has become skilled in its use. It demands a sixth sense, and little education. It transforms and transfigures an audience. I would believe that its crudity kept Valéry away from it. His warnings were of little value.

Valéry noted that the sensibility is the true mover of the intelligence. "If the sensibility of modern man is greatly compromised by the present conditions of his life, and if the future seems to promise an ever harsher treatment, we may be justified in thinking that our intelligence will suffer profoundly from the damage done to our sensibility. But how is the damage being done?" ("The Outlook for Intelligence," 139-40). The life of the senses is controlled by outside conditions. Nothing has become more vivid than human destruction through weaponry. The changes are so vast that the men and women who work with them have become new forms and instruments. They know that they stand at the threshold of yet greater achievements. The senses are dulled by cruelty. They are shattered by television, cinema, and even poetry. Men have placed no limits on the rights to intimate details and nuances. Nothing is too vulgar for presentation. Dictators assign movies to producers like Leni Riefenstahl, to picture the Third Reich with magnificent detail. After watching her films, we no longer wonder why we can quietly close our books. We are now children of the movies. Dictators beg for audiences to which they can send out those wonderful films to be the foundation of education, the training of the senses, the pleasures and joys which come from them. Joy is in sight, it is in listening and in tasting the order that is now running the state: The trains run on time. Valéry remarked that "all contemporary life is inseparable from these excesses. Our organism is subjected more and more to constantly new physical and chemical experiments, reacts to the forces and rhythms inflicted on it almost as if it would to an *insidious poison*. It gets used to its poison, and soon craves it. Everyday it finds the dose too little" ("The Outlook for Intelligence," 140). Should there be a commentary? I doubt it. The best commentary – if we require one – is to reread. The truth appears in clearer light.

Valéry writes about politics with the same finesse that characterizes his writings about poetry. In other words, he is not a political scientist or a thinker whose reflections about politics force him to become a footnote gatherer. Valéry says profound things about political life. These things arise from his education, his writing, his poetry. He knows what he must protect and enunciate. He knows something about human nature. He was educated before he spoke of politics. Man is a whole, a being who continues to be theoretical and practical, who makes separations but refuses to make them absolute. He speculates about them. The whole is slowly discovered in consciousness, in the faith of rationality. "I say," Valéry stated, "that our inner leisure, which is something quite different form chronometric leisure, is being lost. We are losing the essential places in the depths of our being, that priceless absence in which the most delicate elements of life are refreshed and comforted, while the inner creature is in some way cleansed of past and future, or present awareness" ("The Outlook for Intelligence," 142). This dimension of continuation and nurturing which was given to the mind is particularly stressed by Valéry. It brought the statesman to the gentleman. In fact, politics had put aside the gentleman in favor of the power broker, the man who rejects the relationship of politics and morality. Gentlemen don't make politics. They respect it because they know the traditions of the peoples whom they speak for. We wonder, however, if cultivated men and women become the slaves of their gentility and finesse. Gentlemen have not made good statesmen and politicians. Has the realism of the others given us a better and safer life? The gentleman protects his senses from pollution and perversity. The senses must be protected. If the mind is nurtured, then the senses must be nurtured. The cultivation of one without the other is a deformity. We are deeply concerned about this deformity. We know that it can't be avoided as long as we read, observe, and see what is occurring in the world about us. "The dulling of sensibility," Valéry said, "is strongly indicated by our growing general indifference to ugliness and brutal sights" ("The Outlook for Intelligence," 143). Let's take Valéry on a journey into the Russian slave camp, into the German concentration camps, into the works of Primo Levi or Varlam Shalamov's *Kolyma Tales*. Let us not stay long at any such place. Let's visit in silence. Let's look each other in the eyes and make no comments. If we see too much, we see nothing. If we listen too profoundly, we hear nothing. If we are acutely sensitive, we learn to dull the senses. The dullness of intellect or senses is the result of the massive explosiveness of what we see and hear. What should we do? We must see. We must listen, but we don't become identified with an unbearable inhumanity.

We are plagued by the enormity of the noises of the cities, by the ugliness of the crowds, but above all, by the indulgences of humankind, the vulgarities of mass culture. We have entered fully into the era of vulgarity. Every man has been given rights to display himself freely. The new law of behavior declares that in freedom, ugliness and beauty are one, goodness and beastiality flow from and to each other. Valéry observed that "we have developed our museums with a view to cultivation in art. We have introduced a kind of aesthetic education in our schools. But these are specious measures that can only end in spreading an abstract erudition having no real effect" ("The Outlook for Intelligence," 143). Aesthetic education is taught at the university. It is given a place and time. The door is open to it and is then closed. It fades away in the light of the sun, into the darkness of indifference. If reduced to an academic discussion, it is remembered for the examination. From the doors of the university to the street, the gap is profound and unbridgeable. When does aesthetic education become moral education? We believe that it has always been moral education. We have been wrong. Beauty is not justice. Valéry has always been writing moral thought. It is rooted in his devotion to rationality that is the essence of morality. It lays before us the characteristic of man. Thinking is the element of reflection, of consciousness. It must be protected and preserved. Man is defined by it. What would the messianic state be if not one in which men exercise greater and greater degrees of clarity of thought? We enjoy mocking reason, clear and distinct ideas, but we do this only because it is easy to laugh at rationality, to show its practical inadequacies and insufficiencies. Rationality is the jester who is pleasant to have about. The jester must be with us. He is wisdom. Where else would we find the wisdom that he alone provides?

Valéry reminded us that education – after the formalities – belongs to life. "Let us not forget," he said, "that our entire life may be considered as an education, no longer organized or even organizable, but on the contrary, essentially disorderly, consisting of the whole lot of impressions and acquisitions, good or bad, that come to us from life itself" ("The Outlook for Intelligence," 144-45). We have broken the barriers of dualism. We no longer separate radically the good and malicious. We are no longer attuned to them. We hear them in the voice intermingling, playing games with each other. We were deeply moved by the differences of tunes. This has passed away. We praise all sounds. We are no longer able to distinguish one from the other.

We listen to Valéry, not only with our third ear, but also with that political sense which is often forgotten and even is lost among studies of his poetry, aesthetics, and autobiographical encounters. The political drives us beyond our borders, to lands that are different from ours. We need to cross borders and discover what lies beyond them. Valéry noted that "our investigations must be extended to neighboring, or sometimes very distant peoples. Human relations have become so immediate and so numerous, and repercussions so rapid, and often so surprising, that an inquiry into every order of phenomenon found within a limited area is not enough to inform us of the conditions and possibilities of life, even the local conditions and possibilities in that one locality" ("The Outlook for Intelligence," 145).

We are deeply concerned about the political implications of romantic nationalism, of myths of chosen lands and people. We fear that myth is identified with truth. It is the voice of rationality that speaks of the reasonable quality of human nature. It is this same nature that is metamorphosized into dreams of historical rights and unique heritages. Valéry developed a politics free of divine intervention and mythical bluster. This is a century that granted us magnificent myths. The poets laid the foundation in the nineteenth century. We listened to Lenin, to Mussolini, to Hitler, and to the minor figures that kept close to the larger and more pompous ones. We heard their poets. Politics became myth. The myth makers captured mind and body. They educated the senses and trained the mind. We fear the myth makers. They attract us too easily. We want them among us. We yearn to listen to them. Why should we not? They give us visions and dreams. We love their dreams. We share them with others. We feel the warmth of community and church. We don't want this congeniality to leave us. Congeniality is taken away, we are left with boredom, the monotony of existence. We desire the crowd and its faith. In isolation alone is the rational revealed. The senses have a great need of it.

What a wonderful statement of attitude and perspective was Valéry's declaration that "among the features of our epoch there is one I shall speak no ill of. I am no enemy of sports....I mean those sports that do not depend on mere imitation and fashion, on whatever makes a great noise in the newspapers. But it is the *idea* of sports that I like. And I like to transpose it into the realm of the mind" ("The Outlook for Intelligence," 158). We enjoy sports. We find them usually free of corruption. We fear that we corrupt them, but we also cleanse them. Does it create a political view? Sports embody the notion of fair play.

There are rules of behavior. There are judges, umpires, and public judgments. Sports belong to the community, to the nation, but the nation is not its judge. They form a community upon it. We wonder if the community they form is carried over to the political realm. Do men carry what is learned in one realm to another? I would imagine that there is no carryover. The mind categorizes and defines. Each category creates its own reality, blocking off whatever another has to offer. Sports are ultimately a private affair.

We believe that the role of the individual has diminished. Even in the arts, we feel the powers of collectivity. We feel the virtue which has been bestowed upon it. Valéry doubted this. He said that "the individual seems indispensable to any advance in the highest forms of knowledge, and to all productions in the arts. For myself, I hold fast to this opinion, though I recognize that it is based on personal feeling, and I tell myself that we must not try to read the lines of the future in one person....All the notions we have lived with are tottering. The sciences are calling the tune....You know well enough that today, Mephistopheles in person seems to have enrolled them [political principles and economic law] in his hellish crew" ("The Outlook for Intelligence," 157).

We have said this before and say it again: The politics of Valéry is a wisdom literature. Its roots go back to Aristotle although I am not sure of how deeply Valéry penetrated Aristotle's *Politics and Ethics;* he did so intuitively. We know that he believed in an art of thinking. We know that he sought for a higher degree of consciousness, for a freedom which made it possible to explore the nature of the mind. If Valéryean politics is something distinct from the descriptive approach of Raymond Aron, where politics and scholarship forged bonds of union, then its distinction lies in its search for wisdom, for the nature of the political. Valéry sought to comprehend the political mind, the European mind. What came forth from these studies was not a compendium of knowledge, but insights into the truths which, over the centuries, emerged from political reflection. Valéry stands on the shoulders of the sociologists, having a distinct desire to find that consciousness that revealed the qualities of freedom. We can't imagine Valéry giving us two volumes devoted to war and its effects, tracing in them the theoretical works of von Clausewitz. We imagine Valéry as the political essayist devoted to the problems of values and purposes. Valéry offers us those problems in and by which we are driven to find the meaning of human existence. The thinker doesn't merely tell a story or describe an event, he discusses values and asks fundamental questions about our survival, the quality of this survival. With Valéry, we think, discuss, and listen. We develop an intellectual dialogue, always asking why we think one way and not another. We ask the same questions of Valéry today: Why is he saying what he says and not something else? He never wavered from his belief that the individual "stands for the mind's freedom. Now we have seen that freedom (in the highest sense) is becoming, under conditions of modern life, an illusion. We are hypnotized, harassed, stupefied, a victim of all the contradictions, the resonances that rend the air of modern civilization" ("The Outlook for Intelligence," 157).

We move along into the crevices of Valéry's thinking. There will be no radical changes. We are far more concerned with the nuances which express what is dominant and what has faded away.

There are times when I wonder about the Valéry I address. I have discovered nuances in thinking. I am convinced that the Valéry who is constant is the one who loves rationality and who has discovered that it's the only force we have to battle the crudeness of contemporary myths. This rationality is beyond our definitions. It lies beyond us. We are always grasping for it. It is always inspiring us. Rationality has this double flow. It is from this flow that Valéry brings forth his thinking.

6

Féline, de Madariaga, Cornejo

My chapters run from me as if they were characters in a Unamuno novel or the statuary of Daedalus. I knew that they would never be mine as soon as they were written. I didn't, however, know to whom they would belong. I wanted to encounter only the serious reader, the one with whom I could imagine a dialogue. I remembered the friendship between Valéry and Pierre Féline and Valéry's preface to Féline's book *Introduction á un dialogue sur l'art entre un Français et un Marocaine de Fez* (1938). Féline was a boyhood friend. "The two boys lived in the same house in Montpellier....Féline was a talented mathematician – and not at school. It was from him – and not at school – that Valéry got his first interest in mathematics" (notes to "Introduction to a Dialogue on Art," in *History and Politics,* 598). It seems unimaginable to think of a work of art that is not in one way or another touched by politics. We find everywhere in Valéry's work, during these years of the thirties, reflections on politics. We think only with and for values. Suddenly, we realize that the individual belongs to a collectivity, that they work together for a self-realization.

In his preface, Valéry stated: "It is remarkable...that when dealing with a dialogue on art we are reminded of the most difficult political problem in the world today, a problem that tomorrow will be one of the gravest. I refer to the relationship of Europeans with the other inhabitants of the globe and, in particular, with those who, being subjects of or protected by some European power, nevertheless have their own culture and traditions, artistic or intellectual, as well an elite of creators, amateurs and connaisseurs" ("Introduction to a Dialogue" 338-39). We surely agree with Valéry. We have seen this problem develop in the playwright Wole Soyinka and in the poet Léopold Sédar Senghor, former president of Senegal (1860-80). Féline was a student of African culture and one of the most notable figures of French literature. Féline loved

Morocco, married and settled there. Valéry wrote that "Fez charmed him; his aim is now to charm Fez" ("Introduction to a Dialogue," 340). The words are pleasant and meaningful. They can be repeated easily and we do repeat them in many situations. The problem is severe and deeply challenging. How do we approach a strange culture organized as we are by the concepts that have created ours? Do we first steal it and put it into museums to be forever on view, or do we learn more intimately what another culture is by living close to it, moving more and more intimately toward it? There are no well-marked bridges, no roads that are easily followed. We grope like sleepwalkers into the religions and traditions of other peoples. We feel like strangers whose books and travels have only been observations. Valéry knew that it required more. He encouraged Féline to write about Morocco. Morocco needed to be brought to France, but France had to be brought to Africa. The Europeans saw themselves as carriers of a superior culture. They brought the technology they believed was necessary for a civilized life, but they took little for their own. They took ornaments for their houses. "There has been no exchange. It seems to us impossible, and even absurd, that we might receive the slightest spiritual benefit from the populations we have subjected. It is indeed unquestionable that in matters that can be taught, European culture is, in the strict sense, infinitely superior" ("Introduction to a Dialogue," 339). We have much to teach and there are many learners. Our contact must go beyond what we teach. We must be brought to what cannot be taught, to the mysteries of a different life, to its arts and literature, to family and other human relationships. We have no categories to fix. We can often not measure what we see and hear. We have blurred concepts which are changeable and ambiguous. The closer we come to a more peaceful coexistence, the more the fog intensifies and we lose our sense of superiority. There are traditions among the others that fascinate us. We develop a sympathy, a feeling that we can speak of comparative cultures. This pleases us. We need not identify. Thinking makes it possible to read texts, study objects of art, observe the geography, and come to know something about a culture that was never possible for us before. Superiority and inferiority fade away as political and moral judgments. We know that everything can't be taught. "There are products of the mind," Valéry stated, "more subtle than those that can be reduced to neat formulas of expression or systematic methods and practices. As regards these imponderable riches, I am not at all convinced of our superiority" ("Introduction to a Dialogue," 339).

Are we convinced of anything when we approach other cultures? We are amazed by the works of men and women of other religions and experiences. For the moment, I can read a portion of Rabindranath Tagore's *Gitanjali,* or the short stories of Isaac Babel, or a new translation of Homer's *Iliad* and a new translation of the Bible. Printing was a miracle. Worlds of thought now surround me. It is the freedom of choice that designates my being. I am free to choose one book or another, and in another case, not to choose at all. Choice is not made on the basis of superiority or inferiority. It is made on the basis of aesthetic taste. Taste decides. In the course of time, I have learned to enjoy what I previously turned away from indifferently. This development of sensitivity is the essence of education. While I am being taught how to walk, I want at the same time to become sensitive to what I see, touch, and hear. I want to be among different smells and sounds. I want the ambiance to be not only magical but enticing. I know that whatever judgment I make about the objects of my senses is possible but inadequate. I want my senses to lead me to unfathomable experience, pricking the reason, making it aware that it is not adequate for the human experience.

Valéry observed that he "merely wished to suggest that on more than one point, the races we have in our charge can set us some examples. Their life is wiser than ours, and on the whole it is nobler. Though they may have certain marks of coarseness, you will find in them no other vulgarity than what we have taught them" ("Introduction to a Dialogue," 340). Nothing has wounded us more severely, and it will continue to harm us, than the belief in the inequality of the races. Nothing has been more disastrous to us than the belief in a holy land and holy blood, and in the closeness of peoples. These fanciful dreams we see with sharpness and fright in Leni Riefenstahl's films on Nazi Germany. We have found such closeness in Marx and Engel's laws of economic and political change, in the racism that became the nourishment of politics. The search for a messianic figure became the search for a messianic law, or theory of history. Without divine guidance, man discovered the powers of a rationality. It created laws of becoming, recognizing more deeply that beyond the surface of everyday events there was a logic determining the interrelationship between reality and reason. These myths led humankind to believe that reason controlled history, that history was the expression of reason.

A meaningful politics is a fundamental rejection of these myths. They are indeed myths. We may call them fables. We enjoy listening to them. They are games that the mind plays with itself. We have for the moment forgotten Féline. Féline, Valéry tells us, was a "born mathematician and musician. He could teach his Moroccan friends the differential calculus or the art of the fugue. But that would not be making an exchange with them....He studied in detail the composition of the very complex rhythms that predominate in their music and are strangely and mysteriously akin to the arabesque, that astonishing product of the Islamic genius, which learned so much from Greek geometry and its polygonal constructions" ("Introduction to a Dialogue," 341). It is the penetration into the culture of another people that is decisive. We go beyond the surfaces of building, the masses of the streets, and the monuments of history that are carefully noted in guidebooks. Knowledge is the foundation of dialogue, otherwise we have chatter. It leads inward to the intimate moments which are the life of a people. The weakness of our philosophers of history is that they had no blood, no passion for the life of the senses. Rationality is bloodless. The purer it claims to be, the less passion it reveals. Rationality returns us to geometry. We want to feel, to touch, the activities of a people. We prefer a sense of adoption. We want to belong, but never fully. We bear in ourselves powerful forces of love and inquiry. We want to reveal them, but this is never possible where races are differentiated and assume higher or lower status.

Is it a cliché to say that peoples must get to know each other, read each other's language or learn each other's art and architecture? We have preached these things with some success. Nationalism is still the most vital force in our civilization. Nothing seems to delight a people more deeply than the display of power, and the monstrous technology that it brings about. National pride is rampant. Without a sense of compassion for the other, it is vulgar.

We wonder if travel and study resolve the questions of understanding. There is little doubt that men like Hegel and Marx believed that they had created philosophies which would extend from one end of the earth to another. Europe had given the world the highest achievements of the mind. Valéry denied such a cultural imperialism. He knew and feared many of the ideas that flowed from Europe. He felt the dangers of technology and the theories of racial superiority and inferiority that returned the world to the master and the slave, or the worker and the entrepreneur. Theories of history gave races dominance through color and tradition. The course of human history seems fraught with disaster. The desire to bring about change is madness. I often wondered about the sanity of men and women who sought to change human existence, to change the quality of life without altering its economic base. Ideas and helpless constructs fly about in the clouds seeking for a perch to find their rest. If it is a mockery filled with anxiety and despair, then it brought with it a bravery that is necessary for human survival. Serious political thinking is paradoxical and parabolic. We need little else to enter the political realm. Equipped with these, we feel as if we have been given shields and swords. When we think of the worlds they must enter, the battles that must be fought, we retreat a few steps and wonder about the question William James posed: "Is Life Worth Living?" The question haunts us. Answers have meaning only for the moment. The mind is captured by it and refuses to let it go. Each man attacks it differently. Each society gives itself a purpose for living. Happiest are the men who never consider the question.

* * * *

Valéry lived with the idea of a League of Minds. The unity of the Mediterranean world attracted him. It was laden with sources of European civilization. It was European civilization. In speaking of the League of Nations, Valéry spoke of "the creation of a state of mutual understanding between peoples that they may succeed in eliminating from their relationships the brutal expedients, the violent transitory solutions which humanity has so far had to tolerate. The League of Nations then, is founded on a belief in man, on a certain conception of man that implies faith in his intelligence" ("League of Nations: League of Minds," in *History and Politics*, 345). We discover again and again how deeply Valéry identified rationality and belief. He limited this faith to man's intelligence, to place his reason at the service of a cause, the one that proclaims man's dignity and creativity. At the foundation of human existence lies this power to believe, "the will to believe." Valéry made a remark that was dangerously interesting. He identified this faith with the efforts of "the disinterested mind." I have never understood what he meant by this disinterestedness. Lodged in man, it is naturally interested, i.e., it finds meanings in the realization of the self as a mind exploring the mind. The will to disinterestedness is the fundamental concern of the mind. The mind is peculiarly and distinctly concerned with its actuality and potentiality. The disinterested mind may be a corpse. Why is it disinterested? It is not at the service of the frivolous. It is not an "artful dodger." It is disinterested in what is outside its possibilities, what is magical, what is hallucinatory and false. The mind remains devoted to the mind. It is its explorer. It has no other place to go but to the mind. Mind and consciousness are the same.

These words *League of Minds* assume the possibility that there can be a movement from the idea to reality. These are men whose faith made this movement possible. Theoretically, we are dealing with enchanted words. Their listeners are few, isolated and ignored. Their words are universal but often hollow. We turn from them, suspicious of their emptiness. We wonder about their weakness and we despair. Why should we believe if not for pragmatic reasons? Without belief, we go astray. There is only a negative answer to James's question. We believe *in spite of* the belief that believing may be hopeless. The will doesn't deny this. It supersedes it. It affirms what the reason refuses to affirm. It acts when the reason is paralyzed. It goes forward when the reason is inactive and rushes to meditation, to solitude, and to isolation. The senses draw us into reality. There we value some things, adore others, and become attached to many. The senses cause us to love and respect, but also to hate and deny our activities and the objects that live beyond them. The slowness of experience becomes our teacher. We don't want to know *what* something is, but we need to know *that* the something is attainable. Rationality watches carefully. It will have much to say.

If we don't go astray with Valéry's vocabulary, we come across remarks that keep us on the proper tract. Speaking of the International Institute of Intellectual Co-operation, Valéry pragmatically stated: "The problem was absolutely new, and action had to be initiated in an atmosphere of uncertainty. The only way to begin was to do something" ("League of Nations," 345). There is only the individual situation, the players and their cards. The statesman must know what to say and what to hold in silence. He needs the wisdom of time. I believe Valéry had such a wisdom. It came from the imagination. It came from scientific and mathematical interests. He sought the method of experimentation in every activity. Where it was lacking, the mind had been betrayed.

We know that man alone can do nothing. He has no tanks or armies. He is alone with words. These words are precious to Valéry and rightly so. They are a manifestation of what is man's most precious capacity: the ability to love ideas and struggle for them. Valéry noted that we need to create a sensitivity to the world of ideas. We learn to adapt and honor them. This is the sensitive point, the ability of humankind to become conscious of human suffering and the reasons which make these situations necessary. The political thinker is both psychologist and sociologist. He should be everything that the human situation demands. With a tone of despair, Valéry noted that "our Committee on Intellectual Co-operation and of the Institute, labors that are in themselves remarkable and may be very useful, are nevertheless, so far, answers to questions that have not been put, food for appetite that does not as yet exist" ("League of Nations," 346). It has never been possible to organize a large group of intellectuals who could exercise political power. Intellectuals are individuals dedicated to their particular endeavors and rarely yearn to join committees unless it is accompanied with honors and publicity. I find it extraordinary to trace Valéry's participation in what we called the League of Minds. His convictions and commitments are a startling exception to intellectual betrayal. In being this exception, he gave us hope in despair. He refused the skepticism and negativism that led to an intellectual confusion, and a betrayal of the values which constructed European civilization.

We are constantly plagued by the idea that the intellectual, the man or woman who would most benefit from the struggles against dictatorships, are often the least interested in cooperation. There is a selfishness in artistic and intellectual creativity. It hovers passionately about the individual. It seeks to exclude everything that is not directly devoted to his work. It is this selfishness that has brought forth the treason of the intellectual, his willingness to serve the enemy, to maintain his indifference, all justified by his claim to be apolitical, to represent higher ideals. These are usually mere shields for survival, economic and social. There are, however, the few men of character and nobility who find themselves struggling for what they believe is right, men who are willing to go into exile to confront the loss of language, family, and friends. There are men who face courageously the fact that the intellect does have a commitment and belief in a higher reality. This reality is the faith that goodness triumphs over evil. Never is the faith proven in existence. It is rejected by existence, laughed at and mocked. We are reminded of a statement of Socrates who maintained that no evil can come to a good man. Every reasonable person knows that this is not true, that the opposite is more often true. Socrates spoke the truth. The good man, in both victory and defeat, believes that the battle for survival has only just begun, that the wounds of the day become the mortar for the future. The belief in the good is not a belief in the goodness of this or that thing, but in the force which determines them. In defeat, they find that stubborn morality that refuses to give evil its victory. Valéry exhibits a courage that is more Apollonian than Dionysian, more characterized by justice and prudence that passion and love. Kant preferred respect to love. I would imagine that Valéry, without knowing Kant, would have agreed with the philosopher.

We are confronted with a question that we often want to avoid. The belief in the mind comes with a price. We ask ourselves constantly about the price. We ask ourselves if we are willing to pay this price. Values have a price tag. Often we flee from it, or we join with those who have created them. We do a balancing act, weighing the quality of the value. We ask ourselves whether we are ready to defend or surrender value. Fearing that many will act differently when faced with a choice, we fear for the enterprise of values, but we can't be rid of it. If we could, we would lose a dimension of life. We hold values to be vital and we find ourselves in conflict with those whose choices were different. Mention the word *values,* and you imply struggles, even the possibilities of chaos. Mention values, and people rush toward you, saying that each person is the source of his values. We are haunted by this reply that is similar to the one that declares that each man is the judge of beauty and of ugliness. The human mind, however, is not created by its proponents, nor by its opponents. These are groups who praise and condemn what appeals to their feelings. They are wreckers of civilization, imposing doubt on everything we do and say. These conditions are not proper to what we believe. They condition what hinders and confuses the human situation. We can't live intellectually and freely where economics is dismal. Economics is fundamental to spiritual activity. Valéry remarked that "the Mediterranean basin offers the most striking and conclusive example in this connection. This basin is, in fact, a kind of privileged place, predestined, providentially marked out for the vigorous trade that grew up around its shores and moved back and forth between its ports" ("Freedom of the Mind," in *History and Politics*, 195). This lecture was given at the Université des Annales. The Germans would soon enter Paris. Valéry lived with a feeling of impending doom. The noble basin would be destroyed. We hardly imagined a Nazi regime and the depths of its brutality. We rarely encountered the monstrosities of Lenin and Stalin. Valéry's intellectual stance was brave, but it left us with a blindness that is possible to grasp. What was happening, and what would happen in the world of the dictators and their parties, is impossible to define and far beyond knowledge.

We can be struck by the idea that "the mind comes first." We live through the senses. We are natural born hedonists, men and women pursuing the paths not only of happiness, but of pleasures. Happiness belongs to the great man, to the man in love with his work. We admire those people and we wonder if they will ever again appear on the earth. This love of work is characteristic of a living civilization, pride in workmanship, pride in the art of creativity. Valéry, heavily laden with sadness, knew that things were deeply changing. We had too much of Nazism, of Communism, and of Fascism, too many conflicts and racial theories. How much can a profoundly perceptive man absorb? Each one of us has a sense of measure. Each of us is driven to limits. Some will survive. Some will falter. There is always that looking backward and Valéry did it well. There was a time when men "knew how to read – a virtue now lost. They knew how to see, how to hear, and even how to listen, which means that whatever they wished to read, hear, or see *again* was, by recapitulation, turned into a *solid value* and the world's wealth was thus increased" ("Freedom of the Mind," 202).

We listen often to men and women who speak of their age. They are plagued by what is before them. Their judgments are often under-, or overstated. Man cannot avoid such judgment. It is the judgment which relates man closest to self, to others, and to the community. It is, I believe, in Kant's *Critique of the Power of Judgment* that we find the richer veins of Kantian thought. Valéry would have appreciated this text. I find in Valéry's judgments about European civilization and mind some of the most valuable that he contributed to the powers of the mind. Did he believe in the vulgarization of society? Probably. Did he see the end of the civilization that had emerged from the Mediterranean bases?

Probably. He saw a civilization crumbling. Europe brought from its soul the most horrific forms of human evil. Could it have done anything else?

In his answer to the question: "What, in short, is politics?" Valéry stated that "politics consists in the will to gain and keep power so it must exert either constraint or illusion over minds, which are the source of all power" ("Freedom of the Mind," 205-6). The answer has not left us with much. We think of the bureaucracy. We accept it as the most significant aspect of the state. This bureaucracy controls the economic life of the nation. It is its mind. It determines the taxes. It makes possible the intellectual reality of a civilization. There is only a leap from individual to collective life. It is a leap of quality but determined by the leap of quantity. We must consider carefully what these leaps mean. Dictators know that the quantitative leap produces qualitative ones. We can change the nature of man. We can deeply affect the species and we do it. Valéry again and again turns to freedom and individuality. These are his words of salvation. The word has become collective. It speaks of mutual dependence, and organized collection. Individuality is now a luxury. Life is the child of the bureaucracy. We enjoy denying the fact. It reveals the depths of our subjugation. Valéry describes his position well, but it is one that has in no way moved from its fixation with the individual and rationality. Valéry noted that "a man who is not very sensitive to obstacles put in the way of his mind's freedom...will react only slightly against such constraints" ("Freedom of the Mind," 208). The struggle is individual. The great issues of social and economic survival belong to political collectivity. What happens to the children of the nation, the state? We watch and we think. The children move quickly from family to nation. The nation is their purpose.

Valéry made a very significant addition to the freedom of the mind. He spoke of the *rights of the mind*. He knew that this was an arbitrary expression. "These are but words," he said, "that are no rights if there is no force" ("Freedom of the Mind," 208). There is a pragmatic force in these words. The mind must have rights even if it doesn't legally have them. These rights may be conjectures, but they are fundamental to our comprehension of freedom. The *rights of the mind* are inviolable. We hold them to be self-evident, needing neither explanations nor definitions. They exist, what more do we say? We need to think about them. Our thinking is the commentary we make on the rights of the mind. If arbitrary, they may be discarded. If coeternal with the idea of man, their absence is the death of man. There can be no separation between the rights and the values of the mind. There is only a change of vocabulary. Our civilization is measured by its mortality. We wonder about the continuity of its creativity. We wonder about its purpose. We ask ourselves a question: Is it worth believing in? Is it worth being saved?

Solitude gives us a perspective, but it is a powerless one. We need distance for judgment. We live too closely to what we judge. Distance blinds us. We become wary of every conjecture that allows us to think about the world. We despair, but we have little else to do. We return to the past or to the present, and write books about personages, books about ways to be successful in life. We write pseudobooks. We write whenever we have the chance to escape a world we can't encompass in knowledge. Knowledge is weary of its capacity to form concepts and ideas that are more than speculations. There are senses, the common sense that links men together. This is the only means men have of joining together. The common sense is not fixed. It has a history. We wonder what it means in every historical age.

In 1939, Valéry repeated what he wrote in 1919. He spoke in 1919 of the mortality of civilizations. In 1939, he emphasized this belief. Mortality underscored his thinking. It characterized the conclusion he had reached. Could we imagine him saying something else as German troops lived in Paris? Many French intellectuals capitulated to the German authorities and in particular, to the charms of the aesthetic mind of Ernst Jünger. Are we speaking of mortality, or are we speaking of radical changes? Our civilization can vanish. It may crumble. It may have already crumbled. Consciousness of a fact doesn't precede it, but follows it. The European mind may no longer exist, but is this true? The mind, like every distinct human quality, fascinates and confuses us. We mock it. We glorify it. No longer is *confusion* an unsettling term. It is a term expressing the nature of our condition. We live with a confusion that denies us the right categorical statements, that creates the future in the past, and a present in both past and future. In time, we are confounded by events. In space, we are exiled to the unknown, but we take chances. Here lies our strength. We are children who dare to wager their existence on the success of our strength. We are willing to continue the struggle for its betterment. We are willing to sacrifice for it. A point may be reached when this pragmatism will no longer exist. We think back to the philosopher Alain, a friend of Valéry, and we are encouraged. There is a philosophy of common sense, a willingness to balance good and evil, a philosophy of the means that puts aside the dead=mind effects of the extremes of right and left.

Valéry noted that "the mind wants to live in what it has made" ("Freedom of the Mind," 209). There is no other way we can live without distorting what we have called the nature of man, the being who wants to know, the being who suppresses this same wish to know. This being has not often been successful. It doesn't control nature. Man errs. He perverts. He finds out that he enjoys murdering. Man is a strange being.

* * * *

Salvador de Madriaga, in a letter to Valéry in 1933, spoke of man being adrift. We think of man in a boat, traveling from port to port and remaining in none. Man is adrift when his faith and beliefs are scattered, and when running after one, he discovers another. Rarely does he discover another. He discovers that he is no longer prepared for a belief. It seems to be cloudy. It fades away into a few speculations. We lose it quickly. De Madariaga asked: "Are we merely adrift? In any case, we give the incoherent impression of drifting wreckage. What a vast, insane asylum is our world! What discordant gestures! What a cacophony of opinions! What inconsequence! Confusion! Hubbub! Our minds are giving way to an unbridled individualism that knows no other law than its own caprice" ("A Letter from Salvador de Madariaga," in *History and Politics,* 560). The intellectual is excellent as the juggler of words. He uses them with a proficiency that travels far beyond his rivals. He is the powerful storyteller whose descriptions bring us closer and closer to the world about us, but in truth, farther and farther away from it. He holds on to descriptions that have essential worth. He shares with the poet and essayist the capacity to give life to what he perceives. De Madariaga continued: "Yes, I know my dear Valéry, that the word 'humanity' is a beautiful abstraction saturated with sentiment and when it is handled, it drops tears. Find me another, O magician of language! Meanwhile I shall use it, without emotion, to mean all men taken as an organic whole and as they are – that is to say, in intelligent consideration (always subject to debate) of their present condition and their probable evolution" ("A Letter from Salvador de Madariaga," 562). We need a common law between peoples and states. We need universal principles. We need what de Madariaga believed was a universal framework for human behavior. Will men even believe in such a code? Every man speaks of the Ten Commandments, while he attempts to rediscover it in himself. He can't avoid them or turn from them.

Salvador de Madariaga spoke of reaching "those layers of humanity where all races meet. And next, something much more difficult, the method itself must be a process of 'promulgation' also; the search must also be the goal; the world in short, must go along with us in our effort to convert it" ("A Letter from Salvador de Madariaga," 564). We wonder about this search. We are men of exile, seeking to find a unifying principle to which all peoples give their allegiance. This is a very worthy occupation for both men and women who still believe in such commandments. We must assume that they don't exist, that humankind is moved by violence, by that innate wish to dominate. Civilization dominates our sensuous life, crushes it, and makes it subservient to the intellect, but the latter is often destructive of life. It organizes it and crushes its soul. It enjoys killing the senses. This is its great pleasure. Men and women resent this domination. They yearn to be free of the intellect. They want to live by and for the senses. We think of some of the stories of Isaac Babel and Tolstoy's *The Cossacks*. We think of Alcibiades in the "Symposium" of Plato. We think of inebriation and its union with thought. We wonder about the unity which links humankind. We don't know, but we pretend to know. Wherever we find a general principle, it seems to be impossible to detect. It moves toward the concrete, and it vanishes.

Where does it go? We are perplexed. The intellect becomes less and less clear as it hovers about the concrete. It feels unwanted and unknown. It wants to embrace the particular or the individual, but it can't. Its arms are weak and they grow weary. Victory is not there if strength belongs to the left hand. Defeat is total when the arm falls. Neither the senses nor the intellect is man's uniqueness. Man is the child of his strength and weakness. His instruments are bravery and cowardice, violence and order.

* * * *

There are truths which men fail to recognize, those which point to man's need of violence. Creativity is founded in violence. Man's violence has just begun. If what we have seen terrorizes us, then what we may yet see will destroy us. We may be so totally shocked by violence that the intellect no longer functions, nor do the senses act with the vaguest limits. In 1933, Valéry wrote a preface for a book entitled *La Lutte pour la paix* by Mariano H. Cornejo, in which he said in his distinct intellectual manner that "everyone knows perfectly well, for example, that war can no longer be considered, even by the coolest calculator or the most powerful nation, as a means of attaining with sufficient probability a definite end....War of the traditional type no longer has any meaning as you explain so well in Chapter V of your book" ("The Struggle for Peace," in *History and Politics,* 362-63). Human judgment remains extremely fallible when it is exercised in the realm of politics. It slips easily to the rhetoricians, to the act of conviction and persuasion. This is the act dictators know well. It deeply considers its audience. It refuses merely to describe and if it does, there is always a point to be made, an idea to convey, a sense of reality to be communicated. We have created the most sophisticated era of communications. We endow it with a distinct and peculiar individuality. It is an era that makes human beings immediately aware of what is occurring, immediately able to hear the voices of their leaders. The world becomes one. The world is before us. The world is, however, fragmented, disordered, and filled with violence.

We know less and less about the powers of civilization, less and less about the intellect and about the senses. We call out in despair the word *economics,* and we are not sure what we mean by it: competitive, rivalry, "a war of all against all." Is this the key word?

If war had to be eliminated, then we are content that the philosopher Kant, in his *Perpetual Peace,* had made the proclamation. The ending of war is only an idea, a possibility aiming at the progress of humankind. If we think of the issue of war two hundred years after Kant, if we think of the advances in technology used for conflict, we then conclude that war has become an unbearable monstrosity. No longer does war have the meaning that Heraclitus gave to it. No longer are we facing conflicts of logical opposites. We face total destruction. From our experiences of modern warfare, the terrifying faces of cities crushed by the atomic bomb, we turn away from human disaster in disbelief. We refuse to believe that the world can be destroyed, that it is not only mortal, but self-destructive. Man is a being who kills with enjoyment, with pleasure. He kills because it is his nature to be a killer. Cain showed this well. War will never be the same after the atomic bomb. Valéry was certain that we are in a period that has left war behind. We no longer fight wars. We lay waste to vast areas of the earth. We kill massively and take pride in it. We are in a new situation, one that is becoming newer and newer each year. A deep pessimism filled Valéry's remarks. He stated clearly that it may be true that our world is no longer fit for peace. He said: "They bring to Geneva the best will in the world, but along with it, a burden of mental reservations and the invincible habit of wanting to gain an advantage at someone else's expense. *This simple idea no longer fits the conditions of the modern world*" ("The Struggle for Peace," 363). Man can't live without hope. He can't live without believing that his rationality is efficacious. There will be ways to lessen man's hostility to man, one's nation to another, one's religion to another. We cry out in vain about our mortality, but why should it not contain within itself the source of its own survival? It doesn't.

Valéry noted that "independent minds must labor to develop and clarify a conception of politics from which everything that has become absurd, and yet is still practiced, will be eliminated. The rotten past, the *adhesions* of the intellect must be cut away" ("The Struggle for Peace," 363-64).

I would imagine it to be somewhat surprising for a poet to be reading a political study that is not embraced by an ideal, but one that has emerged from a careful analysis of foreign politics and strategy. What he said about Cornejo's book indicated the depth of his interest. It is no longer difficult to imagine him reading such a book and recommending it to others. Valéry accepted the idea that the study of political and economic problems demands a knowledge of facts, a study of national interests, the willingness to explore how these interests conflict with international responsibilities and what sacrifices the national state must make to world problems. These are the difficult problems. They surpass our resolve to deal with them. The national state remains part of our existence. International cooperation is part and parcel of political and moral responsibility. Politics is not without morality, although it is easier to comprehend one without the other. Morality and politics often marry. We find this aesthetically pleasing. We are affected by it. We lose the glow of our satisfaction when we are bidden by the concrete situation to blend morality and politics. We don't always blend them well. A large dose of one cripples the other. It needs cleansing. Valéry cited an example from Cornejo's book that illustrated this concern for knowledge of practical politics. Writing about Cornejo, Valéry remarked: "Your analysis and judgment of the policy of Washington in relation to European policy, have an interest and value that I particularly recommend to the reader" ("The Struggle for Peace," 364).

At the end of a lecture called "French Thought and Art," given on October 25, 1939, Valéry spoke about universality. He said: "I will end by summarizing for you in two words my personal impressions of France: our special quality (sometimes our foible, but often our finest claim) is to believe and to feel that we are universal – by which I mean, *men of universality*....Notice the paradox: to *specialize* in the sense of the *universal*" ("French Thought and Art," in *History and Politics*, 436). We are perplexed. The words play games with us. They drive us toward the particular, toward a craft and its demands. They drive us toward the universal, the yearning to see the universal. We walk away from the game. We don't want to play. The universal is a fading dream never to be captured by us. We want more than what we have learned, the instruments of our education. We tire of them. Our boredom tortures us. We seek new lands and new skies, but practical politics ends our visions. It throws blinkers on us and we are confined to its demands. Our lives have been imposed upon by forces beyond us. Other people determine our actions. Other people tell us where we can go. They tell us that we must fight wars. How impertinent! We have discovered a blinding truth. We don't belong to the self. We are not free. Clio guides our lives and gives them to those fates who rose from Uranus's drops of blood touching the earth at the moment of his castration. They are the three Moirae. Their names are Atropos, Clotho, and Lachesis. We know or should know that we are being watched. They will always be with us, but we don't know what their messages are. Our mortality is our uncertainty. Our uncertainty is terrifying. We yearn to escape, but there is no escape. Politics has become the dwellings of demons. We watch them closely.

7

Dictatorship and the Lie

Valéry died on July 10, 1945. I cite his last words written on May 12, 1945. They are called "Ultima Verba." Valéry wrote:

> Stop, conqueror....Pause at this lofty moment of victory. Be silent for a time and reflect on what to think at this Pinnacle....What to think that will not be meaningless.
>
> A vow, an oath, an irrevocable act, a monument in the soul, and as it were, a solemn prayer: This is what you must utter and establish over the dead and over the living so that this splendid moment of silence shall not perish like any other.

> Declare within you, and engrave it in your heart.
> May the day never dawn
> When the memory of this day
> of victory shall bring
> Bitterness and hateful recollection
> of the present joy.
> Whenever you relive this day,
> May there never come into your mind
> these cruel words:
> "What was the use?"

("Ultima Verba," in History and Politics, 485)

There is joy in peace, a relaxation that returns us to what is happily normal. There is so much ease in normality. We are the children of normalcy. We wish for its indifference to extremes, to the extremes of moral and political issues. Normalcy permits us to seek the least disturbing existence. Others choose for us. We complain a bit. We grow angry but there are other things to do, and we have a wonderful capacity to forget. We do forget. We utter the endless question of despair: What was the use? It gives us no pleasure and no satisfaction. It weighs upon our weakness, deepens our dissatisfaction with self. There are battles to be fought, victories to be achieved, adventures to be undertaken. They demand faith. From where does this faith emerge? What sort of divine gift is it? Knowledge will not help us. We deal with a phenomenon beyond the confines of knowledge. We deal with powers and mysteries within ourselves that reveal themselves unexpectedly. These are the virtues of courage and prudence. Courage lies at the basis of what we do. It must not be cowardly or foolhardily revealed. Courage stands between the act of the coward and the foolhardy. It is comforting to find Aristotle whispering in our ear, helping us to think of difficult moral and political problems. Prudence encourages us to act or to avoid acting. In between these positions there are many subtle positions to which the feelings must be attuned. Since politics and morality are practical arts, they can be taught. Technology can be taught. Politics is learned from experience. More often it is a gift. It is the gift of manipulation and adjustment, of struggle and peace.

Socrates spoke of a demon who guided him. The great leader is guided by a demon. We are never free of demons. They live in the fateful nature of our character. There, they work out their destinies. We are their followers, those of us worthy of a demon. We must engrave within us the splendid moments of victory. They are not often given to us. We learn to reflect upon them. We have the courage to proclaim their glory and the strength to struggle for them.

I think often of Valéry's words. They are a monument to his own life. It is for this reason that we return to him again and again. I return to a story in his *Histoires brisées* called "Calypso." I don't always know why I enjoy this story, but I am convinced that even in a book dedicated to politics, it has a place. Homer said that only one man had not yet reached his home. This man was Odysseus. Homer tells the story well: "But one man alone...his heart set on his wife and his return – Calypso, the bewitching nymph, the lustrous goddess, held him back, deep in her arching caverns, craving him for a husband. But then when the wheeling seasons brought the year around, that year spun out by the gods that he should reach his home, Ithaca – though not even there would he be free of trials, even among his loved ones – then every god took pity, all except Poseidon. He raged on, seething against the great Odysseus till he reached his native land" (*The Odyssey*, 1.16). The crew found their homes and their families. They had lost the interests of the gods. Nothing they could do would concern them, but Odysseus's imprisonment on the island of Ogygia, by the daughter of Atlas, concerned them. Odysseus's fate was an injustice. We imagine Odysseus tired of Calypso. We imagine Calypso deeply in love with Odysseus. Where do we go from here? The gods watch. No human situation is guided by empty skies. Valéry had deep feelings for Calypso. He describes her with gentle and tender words: "Subtly," Valéry said, "she introduced herself into the visible world, venturing herself measurably, little by little. By moments and movements exquisitely detailed, she offered part by part her pure flawless body to the sky, until at last she had declared herself wholly to the sun" ("Calypso," in *Poems in the Rough* [Princeton: Princeton University Press, 1969], 89).

This cunning goddess never revealed the fullness of her subtlety. She knew that exposure was a weakness, that truth is veiled and if it loses the veils which cover it, it fades away. Openness is a dismal fate. I can't imagine Odysseus's ten years with Calypso. I imagine nothing but a love that kept Odysseus away from Ithaca. I imagine a man yearning to leave and a goddess wanting to keep him. Only the gods could give him his freedom. They alone could send Odysseus back to Ithaca. Valéry continued his description: "Yet never did she so advance into the empire of full light that her being was detached entirely from the mystery of the shadows from which she issued" ("Calypso," 89). These shadows entice me. Calypso knew the secret of human politics. She rejected clarity and preciseness. Calypso was never fully known, nor did she want to be known. Her strength lay in the shadows, her unpredictability. Calypso's art was never to be discovered. She fought for this eccentricity. It was her victory over humankind. It disturbed the gods, but Calypso was pleased with her art. She taught the art of disguise, the mysterious art whose truth couldn't be discovered by man. At best, humankind sought to imitate her. She was the goddess of the rhetoricians. They learned their art from her. Her powers of persuasion were overwhelming. No man could resist her. She was a masterful liar. What powers lie in a goddess more persuasive than any man? She brought each power to its subjugation. Each did homage to her and could be discarded. Odysseus had been with her for ten years. No man ever stayed so long. No man had this mysterious survival.

Valéry noted that "it was as though some force at his back restrained her from a complete yielding to the liberties of space, so that for dear life she must remain half the creature of this incomprehensible power, of which her beauty was perhaps no more than a turn of its thought or the incarnation of one of its Ideas" ("Calypso," 89). Calypso belonged to those creatures whose life belonged to forces beyond themselves, to what Homer called "incomprehensible powers." How do we encounter these powers? How do we gather threads of their presence? We don't. We know only that they exist. We discover them in experience unexpectedly. We know that they are present, they will always be present both in and around us. I find Calypso, this goddess of shadows, to be a political form. Valéry's descriptions are far more subtle than Clausewitz's or

Schmitt's or Aron's. He hides the truths of the goddess in a tale and leaves the reader to use or ignore the truths he buries in his descriptions.

Valéry observed that she was cautious, she moved delicately. "Because of her quivering pearly flesh she made one fancy her some infinitely sensitive part of the creature of whom, in that case, her cave would have been the inseparable shell" ("Calypso," 90). This fascinating balance between hiddenness and openness throws us into discord. We are confounded by the movement of the different forces. We observe them. Calypso is the daughter of the shadows, unamiable and unknowable, the daughter of forces. We approach Calypso cautiously, her ability to be only part of herself, to fade away into the unknown and the indefinable. She is, and is always not, what she is. She defies and stings our senses. Yet she draws our feelings to her only to deceive them. She knows this unconsciously. It is her nature that attracts us. We yearn to know it. We will not know it. We may experience it, but never is this experience a full or meaningful one.

Valéry called her "the inseparable shell." We wonder what the shell bore within it. He said that "she seemed a dependent part of this shell." It brought her forces about whom she knew little. They lived in her and showed their reality in her figure and on her body. Calypso yielded an efflorescence that affected everything about her, "upon the dark rocky edges, decked her in quivering festoons of vanishing ripples and folds of strangely sensitive tissue that oozed glittering drops" ("Calypso," 90). We read with wonder these sensuous descriptions. We recognize in them the experiences we have had. Calypso is sensuous beyond all sensuality. Sensuality reached a point of becoming a demon. The demon blinded us. It heightened our attraction. It gave Calypso the magical powers that made her irresistible. Valéry noted that "Calypso seemed the natural product of this calyx, of wet flesh lolling open about her" ("Calypso," 90).

We read Valéry, we hesitate at every phrase, attempting to discover the meanings of his words, the beauty that his words bring to Calypso, the dangers that live in his wet flesh. No flesh is as soft and enticing as that of Calypso. We are open to a depth of beauty never before touched. We are helpless. We have no other place to go. She had no dwelling. Even her caves were mere moments in a life that far surpassed life in sensuality. She wanted her caves, but she scorned them. Her scorn became her return to her caves. Valéry mentions: "For eventually she always retired and withdrew herself, for some reason that remained incomprehensible, and at a moment that no one could guess." Calypso withdrew from the world, but only for moments. She needed to withdraw. Her powers lay within. She needed to be part of them. She needed to hover about "the inseparable shell," but she withdrew from it "as a hand that has touched red-hot iron" ("Calypso," 90).

"Hardly had Calypso appeared and taken form upon the threshold of the sea-cave, than she created love in the fullness of the empty tract. She received it and she returned it with a grace, an energy, a tenderness, a simplicity that were hers alone, yet not without a capriciousness that for her was no doubt a law" ("Calypso," 90). Calypso has confounded us. She is the creator of love which is her divine gift. We imagine Calypso returning the love which is her love. Love emerges from her, but its emergence became its disappearance. We wonder about a love that quietly appears, that attracts, that conquers. This is the love that lures the soul and captures it. Love, alone, seeks to grasp the soul and absorbs it. No longer is the soul captured by love. Love has turned into its opposite, into indifference, power, and cunningness. Calypso is political. She deceptively lures her beings. She corrupts them and consumes them. Odysseus was not consumed. He was her slave. In her presence, she defied the gods. "And the living mantle of her shell was pursed up about her" ("Calypso," 90). We can't imagine the love and beauty of Calypso. They stun our reason, deaden its powers. They leave us silent and immovable. Calypso possessed the suffocating love, the love embodied in the metamorphosis, the love that consumed the soul of its victim. This is love which comes forth from a sinister desire to absorb whatever attracts. Calypso detests freedom. She loves her corpses.

We listen. Valéry speaks and we are tense. He speaks without the Muse. The words don't enchant us. They terrify us, as we know that these are divine words and there is no release from them, but through divine interventions. "At once," Valéry tells us, "every manner of unimaginable sorrow and evil was let loose under the sky. The whole sea swelled and hurled itself upon the rock, shattering and sacrificing upon it a vast number of its loftiest waves. Shipwrecks were to be seen here and there over the breadth of the whelmed water. The sea boomed and banged frightfully in the submarine cavities of the isle, whose grottoes bellowed appalling blasphemies, obscene railings, or breathed forth sighs that pierced the heart" ("Calypso," 91). She had nothing to teach man, no thought to leave with him. She was the terrifying powers of love, the vicious consequences of its encompassing reality. Calypso revealed a nature of love that men have refused and even denied. Have men known differently? Perhaps! We must believe that they have escaped Calypso. In escaping her, they have lost the tumultuous forces of love. Love churns the seas. Its waves fly above and beyond us. We are not passive. The waves are mighty and fierce. We wonder if they will not consume all that we are and will be. Man is defiant. Odysseus was defiant, but what could he do without the gods? Calypso's dreaded powers are beyond human invention. There were times when Calypso withdrew into her caves. We don't comprehend this withdrawal, but we know that destruction needs time and place. We wonder what we are to do with it. It will be permanent. Calypso will appear again from her caves and the horrific forces of love will dominate all that we do and think. Man is helpless when faced with the furies of love, but the furies weary. Man builds his dams, his barriers, the heights of his walls. Calypso is not a unique power. She is ruled by the gods. They loved Odysseus. He suffered too much. Love had weakened him. He had to be released.

She wanted Odysseus for a husband. She kept him from the caves where his freedom would be taken from him. Odysseus left Calypso. His trials were not over. They awaited him in abundance. We hinted that Calypso was a political figure, but we are not sure. Calypso could not be known. "At times," Valéry said, "this ominous retreat was a stealing away, a dissolving as of a reptile from even the firmest clasp; at times she retracted as suddenly and smartly as a hand that had touched red-hot iron" ("Calypso," 90). Does comprehension reach Calypso? I doubt that it does. It reaches into the soul of destructive love, of the black side of Eros, the satanic side. The more love loves, the more it becomes destructive. It confounds and perverts. Love demands limits and when it finds none, it becomes chaotic and mad. Love is both a good and evil force. It brings with it creativity and the shades of darkness. Love bears the name of *Erebus*. This is its dark side. Calypso is the political form of all those who see the world as both good and evil, who see a duality in the essence of thinking, who see the created world as the consequence of an evil demiurge. A politics which Calypso hovers over is mercurial. There are no firm positions. Every form is the source of others. Forms multiply. They are the messages and weapons of political life. No instrument has a permanent place in Calypso's forms. Calypso is the goddess of disguise. She hides truth from falsity and falsity from truth. She drives our eyes wild. She mocks them. She brings madness to everything she touches. Can the politician be trusted? Is truth vital? The great politician is the Calypso figure.

What has Valéry done? What has he seen in Calypso? In her, he saw the union of all the opposites. She gave them form. She was all that Valéry wanted, didn't want, from a woman. The figure of Calypso brought him fascination and despair, weariness and excitement. Calypso was wondrous. She tore apart our comprehension. She left us in bewilderment. We know that her figure belonged both to caves and to the sunlit beaches. In their inordinate loves, men destroy their humanity. Few learned from Calypso. Few learned from Cassandra. It may have been better for them not to learn. We have become prejudiced toward learning and knowledge, but we know that knowledge is not the salvation of the world. Valéry leaves us in a quandary. We hover over it, think about the unknowability of opposites. Cassandra was condemned to know truths. She spoke them to men who would listen to them, not believe in them. Why should men believe in the truth? It disturbs their equilibrium. Chamberlain and Deladier told them that peace would be in our time. War came to challenge peace, to make the statesmen of civilized societies tell us falsities. Falsities gave us the truth of their unreality. We needed to read what we didn't read. We read and heard little. Valéry read. He found what he saw. He showed us the reality of the political struggle, the way to political life and the realization that in every aspect of human thinking the political, in one way or another, seems to find its way. The way had gone into the political. It had entered the realm of the lie.

* * * *

In 1934, Valéry wrote the foreword to Antonio Ferro's book *Salazar: Portugal and Her Leader* (English, 1939). Here we begin again to study political texts, to follow Valéry's encounters with dictators and their extreme political visions. Valéry knew little about Salazer. The dictator is bluntly a liar. He is a builder of fantasies. We wonder how a man deeply absorbed in rationality finds it possible to handle a mythomaniac. We wonder how we approach an experience that is not ours, that is distanced from ours, that is remote, beyond the imagination. This experience is there. It is lived and we have accounts of it. It is an experience that has come into our purview. We speak of it. We attempt to understand it and we believe that we have, but we haven't. The words of the dictator are strange to us. They terrify us and we seek to escape them. We credit them to images. We accept the regime as a whole to the consequence of the lie. This is the age of the lie. We have discovered the lie in a particular act. It has become universal. It is the truth of the lie that we must search for. The truth has become rare and difficult to discover. The lost truth that was the lie plagues us. The lie has risen from the ground to encompass life, to reveal to us the oldest of all messages: Truth is dead, long live the lie! We know that this was inevitable as we witnessed the rise of the dictators. We followed the activities of Mussolini, Stalin, Hitler, and those little ones who imitated well their elders. They all cultivated the lie. They were true mythmakers. They brought a messianic future to simple folk who enjoyed the fascination of parades, of rhetoric, and above all the end of confusion and debate. Society was disciplined.

Every man and woman served the state. It was salvation through the state. It was the lie of salvation. It was the lie of everything said and done. This lie was rational. It developed a mythology that was learned and taught. The lie is rational.

The lie overthrew the world as we knew it: conflicts between falsehood and truth with truth being victorious. It was victorious because science was considered, in its experimentation, its devotion to theory and communication, to be free of values. Valéry was devoted to science. He followed its developments. He knew what was taking place. He followed Einstein's work and the discussions that developed about it. Few poets or men of literature did the same. Science gave his work the balance that is its mark. Valéry's love of rationality was parallel to his love of science and mathematics. The lie was unbearable. It corrupted science. What would occur in a racially controlled state, an Aryan state, if its science was, to a great degree, created by Jews? In Germany, too many physicists, chemists, mathematicians, not to mention psychoanalysts and psychologists, were not, by race, qualified to remain in an Aryan state. They were men who had to be driven out. Years of wasted efforts were made to refute Einstein and Freud. These two names had to be burned out of the German soul so that this soul would be free to create fully. The lie had to cleanse society, to reveal to it the only possible truth – the one created by the lie. A science and a psychoanalysis formed and perpetuated by Jews were intolerable. The racial state had to be pure. This was not an unpleasurable job, it even attracted Carl Jung for a year. It caused him pain for several years. His regrets were profound. Valéry preserved science from myth, from politics. It is the last element of the European mind freed from the oddities of the racists. The scientist is supposed to be value-free. He worked for truth and could only do that. This scientist was a political being. He could work for a racial state or a democratic one. He could work by ignoring the state, but the state doesn't ignore him. We know that the scientist can be bought and sold like every other human being.

Science is the source of a vast killing machine. The technology that followed it made the trains going to the concentration camps operate on time. This was vital to the extermination process. Joining this process was another. We spoke of forgiveness and allowed ourselves to be forgiving. Why should we forgive? Forgiveness was beyond my imagination. Sadly, Valéry didn't deal with these questions. We learned only after his death how extensive was the German destruction of Europe, but we learned even less of the Japanese. They left a heritage of pain and distortion that equaled that of their German allies. We don't forget. If we do, we are easily reminded. In one of the finest books written on the Japanese, entitled *Prisoners of the Japanese: POWs of World War II in the Pacific,* the author Gavan Daws writes: "For POWs, memory was all important. We can forgive. but we can't forget. All prisoners of the Japanese said that. It was the special chant of their tribe, their password, the first article of their faith that what they had been through meant something. Forgiving was hard. Forgetting was impossible. It was humanly impossible to forget what the Japanese had done. It was humanly necessary – essential – to hold the dead in mind and heart. There were some other words spoken like an oath by POWs all over the world, as part of the one big tribe of living soldiers who lived with their dead, had to live with them, and could not be free of living with them" (*Prisoners of the Japanese: POWs of World War II in the Pacific* [New York: William Morrow, 1994,] 396).

Valéry was at the threshold of a new age of physical and psychological disorientation. Europe was confounded by events which shook its foundations, that questioned its rationality and gave birth to every arbitrary and fantastical attitude toward life. Everything was justified. It was called freedom. Everything is possible.

We find our way to "The Idea of Dictatorship." We read the first lines. We find Valéry's ambiguousness to politics. He remarked: "I know almost nothing about practical politics, though I am convinced that it involves everything I abhor. Nothing, surely, could be more impure, more a mixture of things I dislike to see together, such as beastiality and metaphysics, might and right, religion and selfishness, science and histrionics, instincts and ideas" ("The Idea of Dictatorship," in *History and Politics*, 233). It has all been lain before us. Does it depend upon our pleasures and desires, or our ambitions and strengths? We are in politics not because of a decision. We are there because we think, react to the world about us. We cannot avoid being in politics unless we find the cave whose walls hide it. The question we answer is whether we face it intelligently, rhetorically, or ignorantly. The wonder of Valéry, as I have always remarked, is his sense of equilibrium. He is sensitive to extremes, to the gross violations of reason, and to an absence of the moral sense. He is not a politician. He is a statesman. He is a wise guide, the noble figure to whom men and women turn for a modicum of truth. He is neither naive nor cunning. He is not a liar, but we wonder if the lie doesn't penetrate naturally into his soul. Valéry was an honest man. Was he capable of seeing the evils that were brought to our century by the dictators? We say yes and no. It seems as if he did. He knew that radical evil had come in the form of the lie. There was no effective opposition to it. Some men understood it. Some pretended to understand, but understanding brought no meaningful resistance. It brought us the weakness of a rationality that could not control its creations. Rationality fell into its control.

I wondered about Valéry and Salazar. The names don't go with each other. Valéry had never been to Portugal, and it seemed odd to hear him talk about a benevolent dictator. I was interested in what he would say in his preface to Ferro's book on Salazar. I was struck by a remark that Valéry made in the preface. He said, "The ideas of Mr. Salazar as set down in this book, or those attributed to him, seem to me perfectly sound." Following this remark, Valéry went on to say: "I could not without impertinence offer an opinion on the subject of Salazar's actions, being ignorant of them....I limit myself, therefore, to trying to conceive for the reader how a *dictatorship* is possible" ("The Idea of Dictatorship," 233-34). Man established communities and states in opposition to nature. Nature is indifferent. Man is by nature indifferent. He seeks to discover the satisfaction of his senses. The state is an unpleasant necessity that drives man to an order that limits the chaos that is man's natural condition. Man's dependence upon his fellowman comes forth as a need: *I need you and you need me.* This is the beginning of thinking. This is how the encounters begin, how the conversation becomes order. Man is a friend or a devil in need. Friendship is an advantage. Aristotle in his *Ethics*, in the two books on friendship, admitted that man is not capable of friendship. He acts in terms of benefit and pleasure. Valéry mentioned the same fact: "Persons, group interest, sects and parties, each according to its needs and means undermines and saps the order and substance of the state" ("The Idea of Dictatorship," 234). In the democratic state, we are concerned with the needs of the public. In the dictatorship, the needs of the public are determined by the benevolent leader. Men are children needing fathers. Are we sure that the public can judge its welfare through the election of officials? Are we surer that the wiser judges justify what is the welfare of the people?

In a precise description, Valéry spoke of the dictatorship. He stated: "The image of *dictatorship* is the inevitable (and, as it were, instinctive) response of the mind when it no longer finds in the conduct of affairs the authority, continuity and unity that indicate reflective will and the rule of organized knowledge. Such a response is an incontestable fact" ("The Idea of Dictatorship," 235).

Nothing is more disturbing than economic distress and monetary inflation. Germany endured both under Weimar. We remember that Hitler came to power on January 30, 1933. The following month, the Nazis engineered the Reichstag fire. It was called a Communist plot. Civil liberties and freedom of the press were suspended. Germany had become a police and racial state. On April 1st, a boycott against Jewish businesses and professions began. If we want to make a distinction between benevolent dictatorships and those created by myth, we do it not to classify dictatorships but to show that in every category of human activity and form there are significant differentiations. The struggle against arbitrary power, against the blustering forces of myth, demand concentrated and organized strength. The singularity of intellectuals dooms them to failure. This individualism is both their greatness and their disaster. They must fight together with other forces. They are pitiful alone. Solitude easily becomes chaos and despair.

The threat of disorder, inflation, and bombastic and subtle rhetoric, bring the mind to a pleasurable conception of dictatorship. "The vital thing," Valéry observed, "is public order and safety; this goal must be reached by the quickest and shortest way, and at all costs" ("The Idea of Dictatorship," 235). Many would imagine these remarks as a justification of dictatorship, but in fact, they have little to do with justifications. They are descriptions. The problem is suitability. It is a dogmatic and unsustainable conjecture to believe that democratic institutions are suitable for every people, that history makes them capable only of this form of government. There is no single form that has a natural right. What form of government, we ask, is suitable for a particular society at a particular stage of its historical development? The answers dance about us, but never with us. If by chance we are linked with a form of government, then we wonder about the power of being linked to others. Doubts flood our thoughts. We tire and grow wary. We are determined to settle for the worst of the best. This is democracy. Where this is not possible, we live with the best of the worst unhappily.

Valéry noticed that "the same idea is at least latent in all who think of reforming or remaking society according to some theoretical plan, an undertaking that would involve deep and instant changes in law, manners, and even hearts" ("The Idea of Dictatorship," 231). Hopefully, we have often calmed the messianic element. We have discovered limits to its expressions. The Book of Revelation is, however, among us. We turn the pages, reading of grotesque visions. We wonder if this is the religion we have adopted. Listen to a few words from this book: "When a thousand years are over, Satan will be let loose from his dungeon, he will come out to seduce the nations in the four quarters of the earth and to muster them for battle, yes, the hosts of Gog and Magog, countless as the sands of the sea" (Rev. 20:7, New English Bible). We need only imagine the evil forces of the twentieth century. The dictatorships do well in describing them. In the world of the Revelation, we find the upheaval and catastrophes which surrounded us. Our rationality is weak, our imagination limited. We know that there is so much that we don't know, that we put aside causation and flee from its pedantry. We don't know where we are, but we must be somewhere. We need to speak. We must escape John of Patmos. Madness is close to us. We may believe that Satan "was flung into the lake of fire and sulfur, where the beast and the false prophet have been flung, there to be tormented day and night forever" (Rev. 20:10-11). Our imagination tells us something else. It reveals a living Satan, a powerful and incomparable power that dominates, through the lie, humankind.

The lie has returned to humankind with a force never previously imagined. It explodes the work of E. Weil, of A. Kojève, and of their master Hegel. It refutes rationality. There is no law bearing in it the meaning of human history. There is no philosophy of history. History has no meaning but the meanings we want to draw from it or place in it. Valéry knew this well. Somewhat hesitant about the identification of history and reason, between human crises and logical explanations, Valéry leaned philosophically toward David Hume, a man he probably never read. In *An Inquiry Concerning Human Understanding,* Hume stated an idea which is a key to Valéry's thoughts. Hume stated that "in reality, there is no part of matter that does ever, by its sensible qualities, discover any power or energy, or give us ground to imagine that it could produce anything, or be followed by any other object which we could denominate its effect" (*An Inquiry Concerning Human Understanding,* The Library of Liberal Arts [1955], 75). Here we discover in clear language the great refusal to grant to history and reason an inseparable relationship.

Perceptively, Valéry remarked that "politics tends to treat men as *things,* since it is always a matter of dealing with them according to ideas sufficiently abstract to be, on the one hand, translated into action – which requires extremely simplified formulas – and, on the other hand, applied to an indefinite variety of unknown individuals....In any case, the mind, when dealing with men, cannot help reducing them to creatures capable of figuring in its operations" ("The Idea of Dictatorship," 237). We nod our head in passive agreement. There is little else to do. Are we ever sure that it is the mind alone, that the emotions are silent or indifferent? Modern conflicts are deeply emotional. They are often emotionally religious. When they attempt to enter and offer reasonable guidance, we retreat immediately. These conflicts are lampooned. They run from what is seen and heard. They want again to crawl toward the heavens, to find the place of great distances and the imaginary conversations that Voltaire gave us in abundance. There is no escape. We are haunted by reason and by feelings. Men are treated like things when reason manipulates and controls them. They are the objects of logic that reduces them to a concept. Valéry knew well the emotional aspects of existence. Men's hearts must be touched, driven amok with visions of new world orders. Their leaders must lie at the feet of John of Patmos and absorb from him the world of dreams and visions. It is his Christianity that has fascinated and terrified us. The moral stories and the theological mysteries come into play after we have absorbed John's Revelation. Listen for a moment to the description of a vision: "I saw no temple in the city; for its temple was the sovereign Lord God and the Lamb. And the city had no need of sun or moon to shine upon it; for the glory of God gave it light, and its lamp was the Lamb. By its light shall the nations walk, and the kings of the earth shall bring into it all their splendor" (Rev. 21:22-24).

Politics is consumed by passions that determine our needs. It is consumed by what is contrary to our needs, but necessary for our feelings. Religion and politics are the tools of the passions. The heart is far more powerful than the mind. Valéry noticed that in the dictator "there is something of the artist and a certain amount of aesthetics in his conception. He must therefore fashion and mold his human material to make it adaptable to his plan. People's ideas must be pruned... but they must be left, however, with enough undestroyed initiative so that the plans pursued by the mind will not suffer from an excess of submission or inertia in its agents" ("The Idea of Dictatorship," 238). We read these words with surprise and disbelief. There is always a human tragedy in dictatorship. The suppression it brings carries with it a price: limits placed on reason. I can only believe that Valéry smiled when he wrote the following words: "Hence, the political mind, which under all circumstances is the opponent of man – contesting his liberty, his complexity, and his versatility – attains, in a dictatorship regime, to the fullness of the development" ("The Idea of Dictatorship," 238). Whatever we say about the benevolent ruler, about the stage of government he represents, there must be a way to nurture freedom, to educate a people to responsibility. If we choose between chaos and dictatorship, we know that men will choose dictatorship. It is the rule of the family. There are no choices. There can be no democracy without revolution or revolt.

At the end of his Preface, Valéry wrote of the dictator: "He eliminates or isolates all those who will not give up their dictatorial element to him. He remains the sole free will, the only whole intelligence, the sole possessor of the fullness of action, the sole being to enjoy all the properties and prerogatives of the mind, in the face of an immense number of people reduced to an indistinct quantity (whatever their personal value) to the condition of means or material – there is no other name for anything the intelligence can take as its object" ("The Idea of Dictatorship," 240).

We leave these remarks to those who have traveled and bear witness to the varied forms of government that exist. We find it difficult to say what is appropriate for a people, but we do know, and believe, that freedom and responsibility are the foundation of a government of law. There is a prudence in Valéry. It may leave much to be desired. His attitude has been captured by reason. This captivity can be a fault. Yet it is the only truth we have. No one in our age represented them more fully and actively than Valéry. We wonder if the era is over when men turned to reason to find betterment for their conditions, to temperance, to live a happier life, and to courage to make significant decisions and fight necessary wars.

I end this chapter with a quote from Montesquieu who said: "Between societies the right of natural defense implies sometimes the need to attack when a nation sees that to be at peace any longer would place another state in a position to destroy it, and that to attack it that moment is the only way of preventing this destruction (*Spirit of the Laws, Book 10,* [Cambridge: Cambridge University Press, 1989], 138).

Valéry admired Montesquieu. He admired his *Persian Letters* and wrote a preface for a new edition of *Lettres Persanes.* I take from Valéry's description a remark which is wisely significant. Valéry stated: "Hypocrisy is a necessity in an era that demands simplicity in appearances, when human complexity is not tolerated, when jealous authority or stupid opinion imposes a model on people. The model is promptly taken as a mask" ("The Persian Letters," in *History and Politics,* [1926], 224).

8

Descartes

Why do we now turn to Descartes, to a philosopher whose words have charmed and formed a nation? This philosopher gave us an order, an architecture, a collective experience of the *I* that thinks, a universal mathematics. There is an order in thinking and this order has been fashioned in rationality by an explosive statement: "I think therefore I am," *cogito ergo sum.* A simple line, repeated quickly by students to demonstrate the fact that they have learned something from the philosopher. They should never be asked what this sentence means, or why it comes at a particular moment in Descartes's work. Valéry took Descartes very seriously. He read himself into Descartes's experience. He didn't read him to write a dissertation or a scholarly article for a scholarly journal, to be read and forgotten. Valéry wanted to grasp Descartes's original experience, to discover how the mind thinks when it is freed from the realm of perception, how it discovers what is evident, self-evident, beyond historical causation or comparative analysis. In other words, the Cartesian experience is the contradiction of the rhetorical. The latter seeks to persuade and convince an audience through a varied juggling of expressions, through metaphors, symbols, synecdoches. In rhetoric, the victor is the one who carries with him the convictions of the audience. He created the convictions he created for them. With Descartes, we search for self-evidence, for the thinking of the intellect unspoiled by the senses. What we search for is the Cartesian experience. In this experience lies an insight of how the mind thinks upon itself. The mind struggles to liberate itself from what is accidental to it. If we are to think of truth, there must be a thinking that is pure, untouched by sensibility. The method itself is creative of truth. Truth lies in thinking turned to its activity: to think about the possibilities of thinking.

Valéry introduced us to the Descartes who fascinated him, the philosopher of the poetic experience. He reminds us that he himself is not a philosopher, doesn't want to be a philosopher, and is proud of his ignorance of philosophy. We sympathize with him. We find it extremely valuable to speak of a philosopher and yet have no particular interest in philosophical theory. Valéry wrote a "Sketch for a Portrait of Descartes" in 1925 (in *Masters and Friends* [Princeton, Princeton University Press, 1968], 12). In a letter to Gide in 1894, Valéry wrote: "I have lately reread *The Discourse on Method*. It is really the modern novel as it might be done. Don't forget that later philosophy rejected the autobiographical. This is the part that must now be revived, and someone must write *the life of a theory* – too much has been written about the life of passion (in bed)" ("Sketch for a Portrait of Descartes," note 6, 356). Happily, we return to the autobiographical; at least a few of us have. We have joined Unamuno in stressing the personal in attempting to show that a philosophy is a revelation of the wholeness of the thinker. We think not only with the mind, but also with the body. The mind is not imprisoned in the body, but it dwells there as lord of the manor. The autobiographical was rejected for reasons known only to the philosopher. This rejection isolated mind from body, drove the mind to the extremes and left the body in a wasteland, to perish in its poverty. Socrates would have advised us that such separations were artificial and above all, destructive. In the Alcibiades scene at the end of the "Symposium," the autobiographical assumes its role as fundamental to thought. The comic, the tragic, the passionate flow into the rational, the orderly, and the reasonable. We wonder what occurs in this inflow and outflow of reason and passion. We know that man is the creature of both forces, yielding to one at the expense of the other. Never can one be destroyed without the other fading away.

Often in Valéry's writings, we read about his negative attitude toward philosophy and philosophers. It seems that this attitude was developed from traditions within philosophy itself attempting to become more and more distant from life. Philosophy is no longer a search for wisdom. It searches for a distance that separates it more deeply from the critical, experiential situation. It adores imitating mathematics. Philosophy is applicable to something that is beyond itself but this applicability grows weaker and weaker, reducing philosophy to biographical studies. Valéry understood philosophy as an attitude that distanced him ever further from the object or phenomenon he experienced. He wrote at the end of his "Sketch for a Portrait of Descartes": "When it comes to philosophy, I myself am rather like a barbarian in some Athens where he knows that he is surrounded by priceless things and that everything that he sees deserves respect; yet in the midst of this Athens, he becomes worried; he is bored and embarrassed, conscious of a vague feeling of veneration mixed with superstitions, fear, and of a brutal desire to smash everything or set fire to so many wonderful and mysterious things which have no counterpart to his own mind. How can you tolerate the fact that such things exist and are so famous, if the very idea of them would never have occurred to you?...So if I venture to talk about Descartes, it is no doubt because I draw a distinction between him and them" ("Sketch for a Portrait of Descartes," 12). We have always wondered if the life of the philosopher is different from his philosophical thinking. We assume that life is greater than any of its expressions, that philosophy is nothing more than an attempt to think both metaphorically and concretely about life, leaving to others the disciplines, the right to do the same. We enter the vocabulary of a discipline with fear and uncertainty, there to discover that the philosophical builds and forms its questions and images in a traditional and inherited manner. The philosopher has learned his tradition from Athens to the present, salting it with bits of wisdom from India and China. Philosophy is reduced to the history of philosophy, and above all, to epistemological problems, to theories of knowledge.

There is a difference between Descartes, the mathematician, and the Descartes struggling with the reality of doubt. Nothing plagued him more than the demonic nature of doubt. He was the philosopher torn and tattered by it. He sought solutions, resolutions, and was left with innate ideas and God, two fictions which lent little credulity to his thinking. The distinction between Descartes the man and Descartes the philosopher is valid. "Descartes," Valéry remarked, "shuts himself up with the *whole* of his awareness and he pushes the use of his own potentialities to the point of casting doubt on his own *existence* in the very middle of his account of his life!...He creates an opposition between the being and the man. But to be aware of the being in man and to draw such a sharp distinction between the two, to seek a higher degree of certainty by a sort of special procedure, are the first signs *of philosophy*" ("Sketch for a Portrait of Descartes," 11). Perhaps! The problem that we face is how to determine what problems can be expounded by the philosopher more fully than by the psychologist or sociologist. The philosopher may not be rescued if he fades away into the psychologist and sociologist. Let us think for a moment of Max Weber, R. Aron, and V. Pareto. They were philosophers, but they had abandoned the confines of philosophy. The philosopher, if he has something vital to say, must slip away from philosophy. The term *philosopher* is not identifiable with the word *man*. The terms are variables. The terms *man* and *philosopher* are not identifiable. There is no possibility that philosophy and man can be related to each other.

When it comes to Descartes, Valéry is filled with personal details. He read carefully Baillet's *Vie de Descartes* (1691). We read his articles and suddenly realize that we are sharing our thoughts not only with a philosopher, but also with a man whose feelings and circumstances far outweigh the thinker. Descartes becomes a living being who is, above all, a man. Valéry noted that "when Descartes was in Paris, people used to call upon him in the morning in the rooms of the invaluable Father Mersenne at the convent of the Minims in the Palace Royale. It was there that he met M. Métian on July 11, 1644....M. Pascal the younger, who was in Paris, felt a desire to make his acquaintance and had the satisfaction of a talk with him at the Minims' convent, where he had been told he would find him. M. Descartes had the pleasure of hearing him describe the experiments on the Vacuum which he had performed in Rouen. M. Descartes was delighted with M. Pascal's conversation....I am too much concerned for the fame of the latter to transcribe the rest of the story" ("Sketch for a Portrait of Descartes," 7-8).

If we ask what is essential about Descartes, we answer with two words: inner conversation. Descartes taught us how to form the conversation. Man became aware of himself as an *I* addressing an *I*. The dialogue between thinking and the thinker had begun. Philosophy had not emerged unscathed from medieval theology. It was now certain of its foundations, sure of its reality. Philosophy lay in two absolute words. It lay in the *I think.* There it would remain as long as it was loyal to its intention. There it would transfigure the human experience into the mind, revealing the impossibility of knowing without thinking. Valéry observed that "a part of Descartes's aim was to make us hear and understand *himself,* that is, to inspire in us the kind of monologue that was his own necessity, and make us repeat his own vows. *He wanted us to discover in ourselves what he had found in himself*" ("Sketch for a Portrait of Descartes," 10).

Nothing pleased Valéry more than Descartes's ability to create a dwelling that would give him the freedom to become more aware of the self. This awareness didn't shut him off from the things about him. He was immersed in them. In no way was the mind incapable of thought. Its limits were flexible. In fact, thought became more refined and clearer. Descartes sought those clear and distinct ideas that brought him profoundly close to truth, to a formula from which derivative truths ran away incessantly. Valéry was deeply sympathetic to this ideal. Nothing was more significant to him than the process by which truth was possible. This belief in truth became the mark of Valéry's thought. What else had the same significance? I would imagine Valéry being pleased with Husserl's thinking, although he wouldn't have the patience to watch it develop from the pure to the impure. Paradoxically, the search for truth is diametrically opposed to the sensibility, as self-evidence is opposed to skepticism, and incurable doubt. Valéry exclaimed with profound delight: "What a luxurious form of freedom! What an elegant and voluptuous way of being oneself when a man can thus lose himself in things and yet grow stronger in ideas" ("Sketch for a Portrait of Descartes," 10). We speak of the world about us as if it were filled with myriad phenomena. We speak of contingencies, probabilities, and conjectures as if they were the enemies of self-evidency. They are only apparent enemies. In fact, they are friends. Without them the mind would not struggle for truth, would not seek to overwhelm and go beyond them. They are the ways that lead us to the powers of the mind. Valéry noted: "The accidental, the superficial, with its rapid changes, stimulate and clarify what is deepest and most constant in a person who is really born for a high intellectual destiny" ("Sketch for a Portrait of Descartes," 10). Perhaps even more than Montesquieu or Voltaire, Descartes's experience of the *I think*, and the rules for its observation, became Valéry's intellectualism.

How does Valéry conceive of the Cartesian experience? Is there any other way but to see it as the guide to the most magnificent achievement of the European mind? It began with Socrates and ignored Plato and Aristotle. It was lost sight of in the Middle Ages. There it faded into oblivion. The *I* had been born, the *I* that belonged to thinking, that made us aware of thinking, that showed us the way to thinking, that revealed thinking from within thinking. Valéry realized that philosophy cannot be explained. There is little to explain. It is anything the thinker wants it to be. It is politics, morality, science, literature, poetry. Philosophy is an instrument which we use to approach a subject, to reflect upon it, to show its relationship to other fields of thought: to psychology, to sociology, to theories of literature. We say: Let's approach it philosophically, but we are not sure what this means. We escape the need to define philosophy or to make it clear to us. Philosophy is an endeavor to think about something and go beyond it. Philosophy is the experience of transcendence. Descartes knows exactly what philosophy is. In the *Discourse on Method,* he stated: "I was always eager to learn to distinguish truth from falsehood, so that I could make intelligent decisions about the affairs of this life and to act with greater confidence" (*Discourse on Method and Meditations,* Library of Liberal Arts [New York: Macmillan Publishing Co., 1986], 9). Once again we hear philosophy spoken of as if it were a guide to life, a segment of wisdom literature. What is startling about Descartes's approach is his emphasis on "Method." This is the fundamental term, the one that must be explored. Nothing is possible without "Method." It is a way to wisdom. You must learn how to discover it and to follow it. It bears a mystery.

It is the mystery of clarity.

* * * *

In 1937, Valéry spoke at the Sorbonne for the opening of the Ninth International Congress of Philosophy. He spoke of Descartes. He enunciated a philosophy whose thought he deeply valued and incessantly explored. Descartes brought autobiography to thinking and thinking to autobiography. With good humor and impeccable taste, Valéry remarked that he was at the podium in the place of France's most eminent philosopher, Henri Bergson. Bergson was sick. He further said that Bergson "would have spoken to you about Descartes with magical authority, with natural depth and beauty of expression which were peculiarly his." In welcoming the foreign delegates, Valéry with an ingenious sense of detail, remarked that he felt that their presence repaid the visits of Descartes to other countries. He said: "No one has been a better European than our intellectual hero who came and went with such ease. He thought wherever he could think: he meditated, he made discoveries and calculations wherever he happened to be: in a well warmed room in Germany, on the quais in Amsterdam, and as far afield as Sweden, where death overtook the traveler whose freedom of mind was the very precious gift which he never ceased to preserve by his freedom of movement" ("Descartes," 14). We retreat from the Sorbonne for a moment and look about us. We see the world in 1937 that Descartes would never have understood or believed possible. China was falling to the Japanese, Spain was falling to Franco, Mussolini withdrew Italy from the League of Nations, and the Sudeten Germans were preparing to be absorbed into a new racial Germany. We wonder if any of those events were being felt in the halls of the Sorbonne. Should they have been? Perhaps we would be better off if they had not.

In the best of taste, Valéry quipped amusingly: "To tell the truth, the moment I knew they had me caught and bound, and realizing to the full the difficulties and dangers of a task for which I was in no way equipped, I reflected at once on the almost insurmountable obstacle created by the prodigious amount that had been written on the subject. What could I say that was not certain to be found in one of those volumes?" ("Descartes," 15). We are at ease. We are willing to listen. We will not be drowned in scholarly notes. The air will not be musty, the smell free of mold. There will be clarity and preciseness. Valéry spoke as a loyal defender of Descartes, of his worldview, of his unshakable belief in reason and Method. Where Method is absent, rationality hobbles about in chaos. Method is the foundation of rationality. It shows rationality its ways and its forms. When one philosopher reflects upon another, his aim is not to show weaknesses and inconsistencies. We know and feel a delicacy of relationship.

We know that through the centuries Descartes appeared in many forms, although there are certain fundamental assumptions that are always made and considered. We may play Mozart in various ways, but it is Mozart who must appear to be alive in the performances. The emphasis we place on one work or another depends upon the architecture that develops from the understanding of texts. The mind doesn't merely repeat what it learns, it judges. These judgments reveal our search for cogency. The search honors men "who work over their thoughts to make them clear and intelligible [for] they are always the most persuasive" (*Discourse on Method*, 7).

From those who find Descartes to be religious, to those who see in his thought a rationality that will ultimately set aside revealed and historical truth, there are endless variations of thinking about Descartes. We repeat with Valéry what I believe to be a significant insight; "But what greater glory can there be, for a man or a book, than to provoke such conflicting views? The surest sign that you are dead is universal acceptance....A man who had never looked at himself in a mirror would at first glance find nothing to tell him that the unknown face he saw there was connected by the most mysterious links in the world to what he felt and what he thought on this side of the glass" ("Descartes," 16-17). What had been added on to philosophy was the autobiographical. It existed sporadically in antiquity, but came fully to life in Descartes. It was not, like in Montaigne, reflections about life for those who were hungry to further their understanding of what lay around them. Descartes assumed that autobiography was an essential element in philosophy. In fact, philosophy shrivels up. It becomes dry leaf without the autobiographical dimension. From the heights of theoretical speculation, Descartes radically turned to life, and its most concrete problems. These demand evaluation and decision. Descartes assured us in his opening words to the *Discourse*, that "good sense is mankind's most equitably divided endowment....This evidence shows that the ability to judge correctly and to distinguish the true from the false – which is really what is meant by good sense or reason – is the same by innate nature in all men" (*Discourse on Method*, 3-4). This is a conjecture both difficult to assume, and even more painful to believe in. We must necessarily make these assumptions. Without them, philosophy is nothing more than a series of observations, however wise they may be. With them, philosophy enters the realm of speculation. This is its realm.

Nothing seems more democratic than the belief in the autonomy of man's reason, of the responsibility that is given to him, to judge, and to accept the fact that he is a thinking, a judging, and a morally conscious being. In fact, it is in the political arena that these assumptions take on a distinct reality. The citizen must be trained to be thoughtful. He judges carefully and has a sense of the difference between truth and falsity. Whether he engages in political activity or observes it from newspapers makes a difference. At the sidelines, theory is possible. From the inside, it is quickly set aside. The issues determine altitudes. They are implacable and unyielding. We learn to compromise, to find consensus, to crush the irredeemable. Valéry made this extremely clear. He confessed: "I like this difference of opinion among the experts and authorities on Descartes. If they cannot agree among themselves, the amateur at once begins to breathe more freely, and feels rather more disposed to listen to himself and to follow the promptings of his own thought. The fact is that in such matters, I have nothing to offer but a lively curiosity, and I am more interested in the mind itself than in the things that are imagined, argued, and decided in the mind" ("Descartes," 17). If we put aside the belief that we are unavoidably moving toward truth, then we can think of the observing mind, rather than what is observed, of the judging mind, rather than the objects judged. Never, however, can the objects or consequences be ignored. They carry with them political and moral consequence. They affect deeply the social and political lives of men and women. If the statesman studies the process, he is doing a noble thing, but more noble is his ability to do what is just or right in a particular situation with varied conditions. There is no way that we can separate thinking from its consequences or to lift thinking from the thinker. Thinking cannot be put into brackets. It is inseparable from metaphors, symbols, and images. They set limits. They speak of purposes and meanings. Thinking is flooded by pragmatic questions. It can't avoid these questions. They are the natural ingredients of thinking. Without them, thinking is chaotic. Purpose determines the nature and quality of thought. The thinker sees that thought itself reveals the need for order and form. Chaos is unnatural to thinking. Its questions about meaning reveal this incessantly. Why, we ask, is being more valid than nonbeing, order more significant than disorder? We make assumptions, giving significance to one thought rather than to another. We prefer one to the other. This doesn't mean that one is preferable to the other. Our feelings cannot avoid embracing thinking. Why should they be excluded? We are mortal thinkers who can't separate the intellect from sensibility. We keep them apart for our scientific needs, for the purpose of study, of literature and poetry, but this artificial division quickly returns to confused interrelationships. This awareness of the thinking *I* makes a fundamental difference in our thinking. We are aware, and become even more deeply aware, that the intellect is a creative power. It is what Kant called the "Power of Judgment," or what Cassirer called the "Productive

Imagination." We scramble about to discover terms that would explain this unknown creativity and consciousness of the intellect. Faced with a barrage of critics who might both smile and laugh, we offer no concrete proof, but only a Method, a procedure. It creates consequences. We speak seriously of Method and consciousness. It has captured our being, but we resist. Perhaps too firm a capture is dangerous.

Valéry spoke poignantly about the yearning to create, to surpass what has been said and done, to bring something new into the world, into our immediate existence. He spoke as an inspired thinker, believing every word that he uttered. He spoke with ardor. Valéry stated: "The urge to understand and to create; the urge to surpass what others have achieved and to become equal to the greatest, or, on the contrary, the self-denial and the renunciation of fame which are found in some....All this suggests a poetry whose resources are inexhaustible. The creative sensibility, in its noblest forms and its most exquisite productions, seem to me to be just as much a subject for art as all that is moving or dramatic in our everyday life" ("Descartes," 20). I wonder if creative sensibility is anything more than an intellectual virtue, but it is difficult to imagine this virtue without moral consciousness. It is difficult to imagine the intellectual act without the moral dimension. Sadly, I find this dimension often lacking, but then, on the other hand, Valéry worked at the League of Nations. He made it very clear that he had transformed and transfigured his work with a sensitivity for justice and courage, a profound distaste for totalitarianism in every form. No idea was more fundamental for him than freedom. He would have been deeply sensitive to the poets of the Soviet Union and Eastern Europe whose memoirs and poetry made it possible for us to grasp the consequences of dictatorships. If there is an intimate relationship between thinking and autobiography, then we appreciate with fervor Valéry's presentation of his thinking as it weaves a pattern from these interrelationships. We feel both the intellect and the sensibility. We are constantly being drawn back to self, that wonder of relationships that join mystery and intellectual clarity. We are conscious critics in search of errors, inadequacies, limitations. We are pickers of detail in which it is possible to lose a work of art, yet often the detail is the revelation of the work. The mind moves from one to the other rapidly – but slowly – searching for it. We watch carefully these backward and forward movements, fascinated and startled by them, aware that we are observing not a divine comedy, but a human one.

With grace and lightness of touch, Valéry makes a delightful remark which sets at rest our discomforts about the subject matter. We talk little, but yet exclusively about Descartes. We don't mention his name. He is always with us. The reader suddenly realizes that what we have said is a discussion of Descartes. We didn't use the academic method. We put aside the traditional professional attitude and presentation. This would be learned, misty, and somewhat incomprehensible. In these characteristics, supposedly, lie the depths which are applauded eagerly by those who enjoy displays of wisdom. We are convinced, however, that it is not depth we seek, but image, the vision which gives to each detail its proper place in the whole. "Do not imagine, gentlemen," Valéry stated, "that I have wandered a long way from our Descartes. On the contrary, I am still talking about him. He was undoubtedly one of the first and most enterprising of those who have created the present state of human affairs....Moreover, the intention to reduce the effort expanded on each occasion, and to substitute a uniform procedure for the necessity of discovering a particular solution to each problem, is fundamental in Descartes: it is the essence of his Method" ("Descartes," 23). The essence of his Method lies in our capacity to draw close to him, to feel that his experience is also ours, that the more we are immersed in Descartes, the more we are immersed in ourselves.

"In the last resort, to think of him [Descartes] must inevitably make us think of ourselves. This would be the greatest tribute of all. I ask myself therefore, what it is that strikes me most in him, for that is precisely the part that can and must be still alive" ("Descartes," 28). What we ask is the elaboration of this experience which is so essential to philosophy, and gives it the right to exist. What would be more essential for man than consciousness, i.e., self-consciousness? The philosophical experience is rooted in awareness, in the power of the mind to think about itself, to discover its ways to conjectures, to assumptions. This awareness belongs to self-discovery, to the realization that thinking is always the thinking about thinking. Valéry made it characteristically clear what is most vital in Descartes's philosophy: "It is not, I confess, his metaphysics that I can bring to life in this way; it is not even his Method, or at any rate not in the way he formulates it in the *Discourse*. What delights me in him and makes him so alive for me is his consciousness of himself – *his whole being*, summoned to his attention, a penetrating consciousness of the working of his own thought; a consciousness so precise and so dominating that it transforms the Self into an instrument whose infallibility depends only on the degree of his consciousness of it" ("Descartes," 28-29).

We wonder about problems which come to us from tradition and those which are about us. We seem to be born in them without having said a word about recognition. We begin to recognize that there is a serious difference between the problems that the past and our fellow thinkers hand over to us, and the philosophy that continues to grow in us. How few of these past problems are ours. They come to us and demand enumeration in lectures on the history of philosophy. Philosophers gain their livelihood from this artificial history. We are philosophical, it has often been said, only to the degree that we contemplate those problems which come from the Self, those which embrace our being. Valéry recognized a very significant fact: the study of a philosopher involves choice. The interest of one thinker is not necessarily the problem for another. "You will see," Valéry noted, "that I have no great opinion of that substantial part of his work which deals with subjects whose existence or importance he discovered through *other people*....I find it impossible not to accept what seems to be forced on me by the character of our hero" ("Descartes," 29).

If I feel that history is the most inadequate way to come to philosophy, and if I refuse to deny that philosophers are influenced by each other, I turn to the Self, the source of recognition and awareness, awareness of Self, awareness of the other. There seems to be little desire to escape the influences of others and a great desire to avoid consciousness of Self. I wonder if both directions are not always with us, tearing us from one attitude in order to bring us to the other. The scholar-philosopher is a worthy sinecure demanding the collection of vast amounts of information having to be put forth learnedly. If I think of Valéry as such a professor, I laugh. The figure doesn't suit him. He belongs to that honest breed of men and women who have never forgotten the close connection between Self and knowledge. Where and when we hear the cry: Crush the subject, we become fearful, wanting to know what satanic movement is making itself known. It will, in the near future, demand our allegiance to our death. We know that there is no such objectivity which can justify itself without the awareness that subject and object are, equally, moments of thought. They form the movement which thinking allows to them. They bear within themselves every moment that seems to be in conformity and opposition. They are themselves, and their contradiction. This means little if it doesn't reemerge as a human experience. I imagine the words floating about, having an indecisive relationship to the observer and the thinker. Philosophy is significant to those for whom it becomes an embodied reality.

How do we esteem a thinker? Do we add up the thoughts which he has given to us, or do we value him for the incomprehensibility that surrounds his ideas? On the other hand, there are ideas that deeply attract us, cause us pleasure and excitement. Valéry noted that what moved him "is the presence of man himself in this prelude [*The Discourse*] to a philosophy. It is if you like, the use of 'I' and 'me' in a work of this kind, the sound of the human voice; and it is that, perhaps, which is most sharply opposed to the architecture of scholasticism. The use of 'I' and 'me' to introduce us to ways of thinking in completely general terms: that is for me Descartes" ("Descartes," 30). We repeat that with Plato, Spinoza, Kant, or Hegel. We set aside the so-called arbitrary and radical separation between subject and object. It is a meaningless separation. It is arbitrary. Valéry created a Descartes whose reality belonged to re-creation.

Great figures are subject to constant reformations. This is possible only because the figure is great. A poor figure can be summed up in a few generalities. We see in Valéry the mind encountering the mind, changing what it sees. It is changed by what it thinks and explores. We remember with a degree of awe a remark of the German historian Leopold von Ranke, saying that history must mirror what is, *wie es eigentlich gewesen war.* He assumed that such a process was possible. We, with magnifying glasses, are taking pictures of what was and is. We are also interpreters seeking choices, values, purposes in all that we perceive. Does this require thinking?

Descartes embraced values that Valéry believed may have escaped him. He saw a Descartes who was coming into being and would be the source of man's most serious reflections upon himself, the true philosopher.

Valéry stated that the "real Method of Descartes ought to be called *egotism:* the expansion of consciousness for the purpose of knowledge. I have no difficulty in concluding that the essence of *Discourse* is simply the description of the condition and consequence of one event, a sort of *coup d'etat* which rids the Self of all the difficulties, obsessions and parasitic ideas with which it is burdened, but which it never chose nor discovered in itself. Doubting one's own existence seemed to him actually absurd" ("Descartes," 30). What is the meaning of Descartes's *methodical doubt?* Doubt is the firm assumption that *I* exists, that it constitutes being, that it is the foundation of human existence. There is no doubting of the being who doubts. The *I think* is the foundation of consciousness, but not only a consciousness that is wrapped in philosophical vocabulary; it is a living experience exposed in the theater, in literature and poetry. It is the source of history and political judgment. If we speak of man as *Cogito,* then we can answer a question that has stirred debate in our age: Is there forgiveness for the enemy, the one who murders for pleasure and with intent? Can one man forgive another? It is hard to believe that this is possible where there is moral awareness of truth and falsity, of radical evil and the lie. From awareness to decision, there is a leap. We miss in Valéry the quality of this leap, the necessity for it, the willingness to make it. The moral law hangs about us with constant vigilance. It never steps away unless we find ways to avoid it, to convince ourselves that such laws do not exist. We can hardly avoid discovering them. This is the meaning of pedogogy, education for political life. We have learned to doubt our existence. We speak of the absurd. It is a very important word.

Valéry remarked that "the effect of the *Cogito,* to me, is like a clarion sounded by Descartes to summon up the powers of his ego. He repeats it as the watchword of the Self in a number of different places in his work, sounding the reveille to pride and intellectual courage" ("Descartes," 31-32). Perhaps the daring human act is the determination to explore the thinking *I,* to say yes to it, to believe in it, to explore its possibilities and intentions. It seems that nothing explains more fully man's reluctance to use the *I* than the fear that it opens a realm of attitudes never previously considered or known. The *I* bears in it the weaknesses of scholarly thinking, a gathering of facts and statistics which overwhelm the reader or the listener and at the same time leave him unclear about the relationship between Self and activity. The *I* is both the Iliad and Odyssey of the mind. It creates the epic of the *I* and at the same time makes us forget that it is a work of the Self. "Descartes' real wish," Valéry stated, "could only be to raise to its highest pitch what was strongest and most susceptible of generalizations in himself. He wanted above all else to exploit the treasures of his intellectual vigor and desire, and *he was incapable of wanting anything else*" ("Descartes," 32). We come back again and again to the fact that the human activity was ultimately an expression of the Self attempting to know the Self. We say repeatedly: How is such knowledge possible? The question defies our analytical powers. There seems to be no way for an answer to emerge. In the fact that an answer can't emerge, we discover an important attitude. This attitude warns us against logical and apodictic answers. The question poses a possibility that can't be defined or known. What we do know is that the powers of the *I* are so great that we would imagine that it is capable of creating itself. *I* keeps a god in the Self. *I* enhances it with devotions and mysterious capabilities never previously imagined.

With elegance and eloquence, Valéry reminded his audience that "perhaps it would have been better not to entrust to a poet the difficult task of paying him [Descartes] tribute" ("Descartes," 34). The task belongs to a mind that is free to imagine, that is not tied to phenomena, and makes them into new forms and figures. Only the poet would avoid more detailed biographies, more scholarly additions that would finally destroy the man for the circumstances. Valéry remained close to Descartes, the man and the thinker, the thinker who joins with our thought and makes us aware of the greatness of the human mind and its possibilities. The typical problems of Cartesian thought may no longer be of great interest, but the experience of the thinking *I* is fundamental not only to our intellect, but to our social and moral life. It is the idea that opens the future to us. Valéry brought us to an experience we recognize, but with the intensity and closeness that makes it vital to our existence, to our conception of time and space. The *I think* transcends both time and space; it transfigures them into the universality in which the *I* dwells. The universal dwelling of the *I* becomes the source of what we call culture and civilization. It is the essence of knowledge. It is knowledge. Descartes has shown our civilization how to place the *I* above all reality. We believe that it is this reality that becomes consciousness. The *I* is conscious of itself as creator. That is why Valéry has emphasized "the strong, the bold, the great personality of Descartes, whose philosophy has less value for us, perhaps, than the idea that he has given us of a magnificent and memorable Self" ("Descartes," 35).

We conclude with a sentence from *Discourse on Method* which states: "The very principle I took is a rule to stand with, namely, that all things which we conceive very early and very distinctly are true, is known to be true only because God exists, and because He is a supreme and perfect being, and because everything in us comes necessarily from Him....It is evident that it is no less impossible and repugnant to good sense to assume that falsity or imperfection is derived from God, as that truth or perfection is derived from nothingness" (*Discourse on Method*, IV, 39).

Surely it is not the god who entered history that interests Descartes, but the god who is the truth from which reality is derived. It is this truth that he seeks. It is this truth that he needs, although he would never admit this pragmatic need. It is subjective and therefore varies in its possibilities. However, it is only the god of need that is essential. We need to know that the world lies on a foundation of truth, that truth is beyond, but also the foundation of choices. Truth imposes itself upon us. It makes it possible to undertake that powerful journey to god, knowing that in all that we do and think the divine is present as truth, causing us to go forward in our images and searches. More precious than any god of the religions is this truth that makes reality a way to discover the difference between truth or falsity. The presence of truth may not need the word *god*. It is what it is: the most powerful idea ever granted to man or the most hollow and superficial one.

9

The Demoniacal

There is no more effective way of comprehending the foundation of Valéry's thought than by a continuing study of Descartes. Study means reading and, above all, rereading both Descartes's and Valéry's texts. No man or woman studies these two thinkers with the detail necessary for a clear and precise point of view, grasping the powerful identification between them. There is at the end of Valéry's essay on Descartes a statement that is deeply characteristic of Valéry's thought. He stated: "For it is possible, after all, that man born to achieve greatness must become deaf, blind, impervious to everything, even truths and realities, which are liable to cut across his aims, his impulses, his destiny, his way of growth, his inward life, his own world-line" ("Descartes," 32). We have heard such statements before. They reveal not only the power of the intellect, but also the power of the will. We feel the depths of the emotion and the meaning of the intellect. We are no longer scattered in our interests, no longer confused and uncertain. We have found a central point, a point of reference. It is a magnetic point around which the multiplicity of our interests gather. They are collected by the *I think.* They are ordered and take on form. We observe with fascination how the mind creates its architecture. We are not only observers, but thinkers. We send the mind in different directions, but we do this only to the degree that we have already some knowledge of where we are going. The mind is controlled by the *I,* but this is only the beginning of the story. We wonder about the unexpected, the unknown, and the arbitrary. We are assured of only one fact: God exists. This existence gives stability to the world. Its idea has been implanted in us. The idea is called God. God is not revealed in history. He is revealed in the fact that existence is not absurd, that history is not absurd. This is truth from the human point of view. In view of the presence of God in our thought, we reject the notion of absurdity.

In 1941, Valéry published "A View of Descartes" as a preface to *Les Pages immortelles de Descartes choisies et expliquées*. Wherever we turn in Valéry's writing about Descartes, we find no fundamental change of attitude. We find nuances of valuation. We find that never-ending belief that in Descartes there lies a significant, and perhaps the most significant, philosophical experience. We discover what we have always known: Descartes more than any other figure in poetry, science, literature, and philosophy revealed the nature of the *I think*. In this experience, Descartes opened to us the vast potential of the mind, and at the same time, made it possible for us to explore a "Method" which made it possible to think about the workings of the mind. In speaking of Descartes's student days, Valéry remarked: "He observed that nothing was too strange or too incredible to have been taught by one philosopher or another. This intellectual shock was an event of capital importance in the development of his mind. It occurred about the age of sixteen....His whole career can be regarded as the development of this self-realization which was to change into a powerfully creative reaction under the impetus of a second inner event, seven years later" ("A View of Descartes," in *Masters and Friends*, 37).

Referring to the varied forms of knowledge, to their claims to contain within them truths which they alone would reveal, Descartes knew that he faced the falsities of those who profess to know what, in truth, they didn't know. He remarked in the opening pages of the *Discourse*: "I thought I knew enough of the disreputable doctrines not to be taken in by the promises of an alchemist, the predictions of an astrologer, the impostures of a magician , or by the tricks and boasts of any of those who profess to know that which they do not know" (*Discourse on Method*, I, 9). Here we find the keys to a revolutionary belief, one which changes our view of philosophy, and our evaluation of the idea of man. Suddenly, Descartes became aware of a basic situation: His studies didn't lead to truth. In fact, they blinded him. He knew many things about history, language, philosophy. He knew that they were fantasies capable of enlightening the world, but providing no truth about it. Valéry noted with firm conviction Descartes's remark that "now, mathematics apart, I see that all the rest is simply a pastime, or completely worthless" ("Descartes," 38). It indicates that, like Luther, Descartes believed that he had brought about a revolution in human thought, that he had brought it back to its beginnings, to its primordial truth, the truth of the *I think*, one that no other being but man utters. This is the expression of man's peculiar self-consciousness. Luther broke through the hierarchical architecture of the Roman Church with doctrine which he elaborated in the Ninety-five Theses (1517), "The Freedom of a Christian" (1520), and in a political text of great importance, "Temporal Authority: To What

Extent It Should Be Obeyed" (1523). Luther was more than a reformer. Reformers don't make revolutions. The old doctrine has to be overcome and a radically new one takes its place. Luther created a new faith that would forever live beside the old and deprive it of its universality. Luther became the thorn which would always bleed in the body of the Roman Church. Valéry was no such thinker or believer, but he was revolutionary in his experience of Descartes. He brought Descartes into his own century, not merely to show parallels, but to reveal the nature of the primordial truth of being. This truth speaks the same words that were spoken at the burning bush: "I am that I am." The *I think* can say nothing of itself but: "I think thus I am." I see little difference in these two expressions. They express the circular nature of thinking. The circle is sacred. It expands into reality, transforms it, and returns it to the *I think.* God spoke to the radical nature of God. Descartes and Valéry spoke the same words from a mind created in the image of the divine.

We witness a "sudden abolition of all the privileges of authority, the declaration of the nullity of all traditional teaching, the institution of a new inner power based on self-evidence, doubt, 'good sense,' the observation of facts, the rigorous formulation of arguments – this ruthless cleanup of the mental laboratory amounted, in 1619, to a series of extraordinary measures adopted and decreed in his winter solitude by a man of twenty-three, confident in his own speculations and convinced of their validity in which he found the same strength as in the very sense of his own existence" ("A View of Descartes," 40). Valéry goes on to compare a scene one hundred seventy years later in a room in Valence where the young Napoleon, an artillery officer, experienced a self-realization that was to mark his destiny. We think of Valéry standing between Descartes and Napoleon, between the clearest expression of human thinking and its endless self-realization, and one of the greatest strategists known to our civilization, the man of action always needed by the man of solitude.

We feel a magical tone in Valéry's words. It is as if he had found his true dwelling, having put aside so many of his interests to enter these halls of truth which he alone had been asked to join. He seems astounded and fascinated by the discovery, something he searched for his whole life. He sought to find Descartes at every stage of his development, just as he sought to discover himself in 1892 in Genoa. Of this experience, Valéry remarked: "At the age of twenty I had to take very seriously measures against Idols in general. At first, it was a matter of only one that obsessed me, making life almost unbearable. The power of absurdity is unbelievable" (notes to "A View of Descartes," 361).

We think back to the startling statement which Valéry uttered on that night of November 9, 1892: "My whole fate is being played out in my head." This is the startling experience of the thinker who discovers a path that leads him from chaos and doubt to the realization that absurdity is not the definition of life. The encounter with absurdity bears in it a trembling and a fear, the distortions of existence. Descartes was so deeply startled by what had occurred to him on November 10, 1619, that he began to pray and made a vow to go on a pilgrimage "in order to place the affair, which he regarded as *the most important of his life, under the protection of the Blessed Virgin*" ("A View of Descartes," 41). The reader reads with fascination these experiences. Very often he is silent. There is little that he can say. He may speak of appreciation and admiration, but the distance between the reader and the event is vast and unbridgeable. These are unique experiences linking the intellect to sensibility in such a way that we create relationships between thought and feelings, without weakening one in favor of the other. How well Valéry was able to grasp Descartes's experience! He was prepared for it. He was sensitive to it. This preparation and sensitivity brought Descartes to Valéry, perhaps as close as the young Valéry felt to Mallarmé or Féline. He knew what had happened to Descartes. He, unlike the historian or the philosopher of history, empathized with Descartes. There is a great difference between having knowledge of something or someone and being spiritually and emotionally tied to them through similarity of feeling and attitude. He understood what Baillet said: "He had so wearied himself that his brain caught fire and he fell into a sort of enthusiasm, which so affected his already prostrate mind as to put it into a condition to receive the impression of dreams and visions" ("A View of Descartes," 41).

The reader is driven by the search for mystery. He reads of these amazingly magical events. He is fascinated, but he is also confused. They have never occurred in his own existence. He begins to wonder if they did truly occur with the fervor that they are described. He wonders if he may have undergone such an experience, but never recognized it. There are always degrees of intensity, moments of exaggeration and even moments of neglect. More could have occurred than was recognized. It is always a question of recognition, and the preparation that must accompany it. We wonder about Descartes's daimon, this inner power that is so alive in him, the one that has driven him from his scholastic studies, caused him to doubt his being and to think of the absurdity of self. "He asks heaven," Valéry remarked, "to confirm him in his conception of a method of rightly conducting his *reason,* yet this method required a fundamental belief and confidence in *himself,* for these were the conditions required to destroy confidence and belief in the authority of the doctrines of tradition" ("A View of Descartes," 43). The distance between the Self and the Self of another may be very narrow. We learn how to approach the other. It requires more than recognition, more than the sounds of words, more than an I-Thou relationship. It demands sensitivity to the madness which accompanies separation. It demands the overcoming of doubt. These are slow, very slow, achievements, rarely achieved by the individual. Valéry's genius lay in this capacity to approach a mind that was in many ways similar to his. We are amazed by the confidence in Self, this rare and unique capacity to believe in Self. Speaking of Descartes's certainty, Valéry observed that "he [Descartes] must be under some illusion about its reality; finally after so much faith in himself, an appeal to the faith that he had received from the Church and through grace" ("A View of Descartes," 43).

Valéry found comfort in telling his readers that he was not a philosopher, but I am sure that he knew that with these words he was making a philosophic statement, beginning a life-long debate with philosophy. He meant that he was not interested in philosophical abstraction, in the logic of concepts, or in any philosophy that didn't explore man's capacity to create, to change what lay in him or about him. In thinking about these realms, thought changes them. It discovers itself. It seeks to go forward and rediscover a realm already known to the senses. This is man's unique place in the universe. Not being a professional philosopher doesn't deny the thinker the need to speak of experiences which he wants to comprehend and needs to examine. Valéry mentioned that not being a scholar of Descartes "still enables me, when I think them over, [his observations] to discover in those very precious and dramatic moments a more real interest and a greater *present* importance, or rather *eternal presence*, than anything I can find in the examination and discussion of the Cartesian metaphysics. His metaphysics, like many another, has not and can no longer have anything but an historical importance" ("A View of Descartes," 44). Every attempt to find an identification with a previous philosophical system ends in failure. Yet the attempt is made again and again to repeat Plato, or Hume, or Kant, or above all Hegel. Failure is inevitable. Time, the master of our thinking, has changed the place from which we think. How would Descartes respond to World War II, to the dictatorships, to the ideologies? We wonder, with a smile, at the depths of the abyss that separates us. We still speak of Descartes because certain experiences have remained constant, although the circumstances are radically changed. We do speak to Descartes through the *I think,* through its meaning for us. This is a changeless truth in ever-changing circumstances.

We return again to that fascination which forces us to seek in Descartes the primordial experience of self-thinking. Perhaps no philosopher has identified the Self with thinking as did Descartes. Three centuries later, it would be recognized by Valéry as the most important philosophical discovery of the European mind. Descartes allows us to watch the nature of its birth. He brings us with him in his *Discourse*. We watch as the birth takes place, as a philosopher brings forth a thinking hardly imaginable in medieval scholasticism. Socrates told us of his external activities. Alcibiades filled in the details. In autobiography, Descartes found a way to communication. We understood it quickly. Valéry described what he thought was fascinating to observe: "the inner Proteus passing from rigidity to intoxication, asking of prayer the strength to persevere in the way of rational thinking, begging divine persons to support him in the proudest of enterprises, and finally producing some exceedingly obscure dreams as evidence in favor of his system of clear thought....There is no other [philosopher] whose character, meaning the reaction of the whole man, participates more actively in the production of abstract thought" ("A View of Descartes," 45). This judgment of Valéry was powerfully necessary for him. He built philosophy upon the experiencing *Cogito*. I imagine that it was only William James who would have seen so clearly into the Cartesian experience, if he had read him carefully, and was sensitive to this relationship between thinking and autobiography. The mind struggled to find a "Method" by which it could submit all reality and comprehend it from a universal perspective. This would be the achievement of a universal mathematics, a unified knowledge capable of uniting humankind into a republic of knowledge, an ideal that causes us to smile. The absurdity that we refused to identify with the Self can now no longer be avoided. We no longer have to travel through centuries to realize how radically changes take place. We look at the events and we see a chimera. We often don't know what they mean, but we have the feeling that what occurred before the event will be vastly different from what will occur after it. We remember that in June 1940, France concluded an armistice with Germany. The event is overwhelming and decisive, perhaps as decisive as the German invasion of the Soviet Union or Mr. Churchill becoming Prime Minister. We have events, personalities, contingencies, and accidents. We attempt to add them up. We get no total. We have visions of absurdity. We are not sure of any meaning. We think of chaos. We are unsure. Valéry remarked that "Descartes' aim was nothing less than to arrive at a *view of all things* which would enable him to apply his method to them, and in such a way that he could reason about them with the same boldness and confidence as a geometer could once he had settled his definitions, drawn up and stated his axioms and postulates, and so found the paths to a particular truth as it were, predetermined and unfolding in front of him" ("A View of Descartes," 50).

Easily we turn to the opinion of "the experts," the men and women who, allegedly, have learned how to analyze situations, attitudes, and facts. Since there is much confusion among "the experts," we wonder if they will ever find a "Method" capable of clarity and preciseness. Is such a "Method" necessary? What would occur if we realized that objects of politics would deny any attempt to give them order? Politics lives from disorder, from the lie, from the confused and the arbitrary. Must the thinker leave politics aside or surrender it to a fatalism unique to its being? There it would be a part in the vast arena of human life. The philosopher gazes upon it. He would immediately return to his podium and speak abstractly of philosophical systems or the history of philosophy. This would require the tradition, not the *Cogito.*

Valéry was rightly convinced that "the whole of Descartes's intellectual life was inspired by the idea of creating and imposing on everything belonging to the realm of knowledge a uniform method of treatment that would turn every question into a particular form of geometric space" ("A View of Descartes," 51). Men from the age of Plato, from his *Republic,* have sought in one way or another to find a hierarchy of laws ending in God, the Supreme Lawgiver. Plato, in the *Laws,* reminded us that God was the measure of being. We remember the stature of both Solon and Lycurgus, the lawgiver. We never avoid the great lawgiver Moses. Even as Christianity pulled away from Judaism, it formed a new expression of the law, now combined with Roman law. The Church called it Canon Law. From the imposition of law to the imposition of the postulates and axioms of geometry and ethics, little seemed to change. Things did radically change. The mind didn't discover this truth. It was not given to it. God supposedly determined its existence. It claimed to be derived from his truth and whatever followed, universal law, divine law, human law, were the consequences of a first and primordial truth: God's existence. Never was one identified with another, but each was derived from the other. This meant that there was a recognition that law in the pyramidal hierarchy contained moments of freedom, undetermined by the order. "A mind," Valéry said, "prepared to commit all its powers to this vital undertaking, must be freed from worldly cares....Descartes, therefore, devised a policy of caution, even of mistrust" ("A View of Descartes," 52). Descartes assumed an attitude that he, Valéry, deeply admired. It was the attitude of the Jesuit. It was a sense of obedience to the Self, of trust and utter determination. Descartes absorbed more from the Jesuits than he was willing to admit. Valéry, sadly, made no reference to them. The *Spiritual Exercises* is a philosophical text combining autobiography with thought and feeling, with an immanent sense of the presence of God. "Once and for all,

Descartes took up a firm stand against anything that could distract him from his great design" ("A View of Descartes," 52).

Descartes had imbibed well from his teachers, more than he would admit. He easily, however, discarded the materials which filled their scholarly lectures. He said to the Church that he would follow their dictates. He had no better ones. He needed, like every man, a guide to salvation. Salvation had not yet been forgotten. But his own work would be hindered by no external force or interest. He believed firmly in the truth that lay in him, a truth that had a divine origin and that could not be spoken of without the divine power to implant ideas in the human soul. "Descartes," Valéry mentioned, "had settled his accounts with philosophy – the philosophy of other people. He had planned or worked out his own personal way of life. He had complete confidence in his own armory of mathematical models and ideals...without regard to any tradition, to engage in the struggle: the struggle of his own will to clarify and organize knowledge against the uncertain, the haphazard, the muddled, the inconsequential, which are the likeliest attributes of most of our thinking" ("A View of Descartes," 53). The truth that is free of circumstance, that can stand over and above political and economic events, is the *Je pense donc je suis*. This is the fundamental law of the intellect. This is the truth of the intellect. It is its substance, its potentiality, and its expression. We wonder if thinking belongs in any way to circumstances, to the fleeting occurrences that make up our daily activities of self-cares. This *Je pense* demands our constant concern. We nurture it. We struggle to separate it from the senses. We seek purity. Kant inherited that word. We metamorphosize it, seeing it as the foundation of human thought, the definition of man.

Descartes announced to the world that "he was a substance "whose whole essence was to think, a substance entirely independent of body, place and every material thing" ("A View of Descartes," 5). There will always be those who will artfully dismiss Descartes's autobiographical references. They do that at the expense of understanding how profoundly autobiography and thinking belong to each other. I am saying that there is a necessary link between them. The link is probative. It is significant. It grows stronger and unbreakable when we realize that the thinking subject consciously struggles to be free of the body, to think above and beyond it, to be conscious of the fact that thinking is always an emergence of Self, more and more conscious of itself, as *I think*. Nothing previously in the realm of philosophy experienced such a powerful penetration into the *I* that creates from within itself what we call reality: science and mathematics. We leave the other fields of human endeavor to evaluation, i.e., to judgment. The *I think* is active there with a highly developed sense of insight, intuition, and sensitivity. We read

Descartes and, when we are finely attuned by Valéry's judgments, we realize that philosophy is not the history of philosophy, but the experience of it. We are fascinated, and often startled, watching one mind conversing with another, sharing a mutual participation in thinking, conscious of the *I* as the substance of all thought. Thought has been drawn from the heavens. God has fallen from his heavenly realm and found a dwelling in man's *I think*. Happily, his priests can still lead Descartes to his salvation. The philosopher believes that he has clearly and precisely separated the soul from the body and leaves us with two distinct realms that we find difficult to keep apart from each other. They seem to have a natural affection for each. They fret about their separation. They also, at times, enjoy the division, each happy to have parted from the other. We enjoy this interminable struggle.

Valéry noted that at this point in his thinking about Descartes, he was going to be bold in his interpretation. Speaking of the *I think, therefore I am*, Valéry said: "I say that we can consider it from a very different point of view – we can assert that this brief and pregnant expression of its author's personality *has no meaning whatsoever*. But I must add that it has *a great value*, entirely characteristic of the man himself. I maintain that the *Cogito ergo sum* has no meaning because that little word *sum* has no meaning" ("A View of Descartes," 54). If we take seriously the *Cogito*, and there is no way that we can't, then philosophy becomes the deepest conscious human experience from which no thought is absent. The *Cogito* accompanies thinking, it creates an inner conversation between itself and the object of its speculation. Philosophy has set aside its ancillary occupations: logic, epistemology, ethics. It avoids the quicksand that lies in the never-ending studies of the history of philosophy which is more a study of the history of culture than it is of philosophy. Descartes returned philosophy to its unique and primordial experience, the experience of thinking about thinking. In this experience, the thinker becomes a philosopher. Where this experience is absent, the thinker has faded away. He speaks an everyday language of desire and acquisition, a commercial language of mine and yours. Valéry spoke of Descartes taking up "the theme of the lucid Self; it is the clarion call to his pride and the resources of his being" ("A View of Descartes," 56).

Descartes dared to say *I*, a magnificent act of courage that few of us indulge in, that few of us would risk or have the confidence to say. Where the risk is small or the company particularly private, we risk the *Cogito*. The *Cogito* is more than an instrument of knowledge, a guide to higher principles, to a divine revelation. The *Cogito* is not a spiritual truth. It is an experienced one. It is the truth from which man studies his being. The *Cogito* is alive in every act of the play that Descartes wrote as he moved from universal doubt, to dreams, to daimons. He loved to pretend. He knew that the Self needed more than lapidary sentences to nurture its experience. Its language needed to be descriptive and imaginary. The *Cogito* demanded an inventive language. It is not handed down. It is not a traditional formula such as the Socratic statement that "the unexamined life is not worth living." The *Cogito* is the immanent experience of thinking. Descartes knew how easily we were attracted by epigrams that are handed down from generation to generation. If, by chance, the *Cogito* would be hidden in such an epigram, it would lose its reality. It would fall to the wayside, there to be picked up and discarded. We smile as we read in the *Discourse* how Descartes suspended judgment. He feared the evil demon, The Deceiver, that would distort and cripple his thinking. Valéry speaks of that famous night of November 10, 1619, of the Genius "who foretold the dreams before he went to bed, an evil Genius to whom he attributed a pain that woke him and the intention to lead him astray" ("A View of Descartes," 59). Luther had his devil. Descartes had his. I wonder if any great thought exists without the devil. We try to change the name. There is despair, fear, trembling, and a host of other terms which afflict the thinker. Descartes grasped the powers of doubt. They tormented him. He knew that he would overcome, that there was a truth in him. Belief saved his speculations. It is a belief we all depend upon. It is our fortress of certainty. This is the battle of Gog and Magog. This is the eternal battle from which we are never liberated.

The Great Deceiver lay in wait for Descartes at every step of his thinking. Descartes was too important a thinker to be handed over easily to his most serious rival: absurdity. Descartes was plagued by uncertainty and haunted by doubt. Valéry asked: "How could he rid himself of a doubt so absolute and so resourceful? So far as his existence was concerned, he had already outwitted and defied The Deceiver by his magic formula of incantation. *I am, I exist.* But the question now was to find a way of proving that everything else, his body itself and the word, either was or could be just as existent as himself" ("A View of Descartes," 59-60). The Cartesian struggle expands into every human activity. It is futile to separate every Cartesian argument for precise analysis and consistency. It is futile to give them a greater order than they possess. There lies in all that Descartes said the ever-presence of the demons. They attempt to draw God into a system of beliefs that is derived from him and that justifies the notions of perfection and truth. There is no way of knowing if the one who is called God doesn't possess satanic deception. There is no reason to believe that God is pure goodness and justice. The deceiving God is as powerful and significant as the so-called good and just God. We wonder if these problems held Descartes's interest in the years after 1619. The mind, whatever be its problems, is always moving backward and forward, searching in itself for the realities it encounters. It is always the fire approaching the wax, the fascinations and metamorphoses that move our consciousness from experience to experience. Never can we avoid the *Cogito*. It identifies man, but is never identifiable with him. Dictatorial regimes create fascinating identifications. Religious traditions follow close by, and remembrances of things past falsify the mind in its awareness of Self. There are things we struggle to stay away from, and are happy to be disengaged from. We can live with Descartes' experience. We cannot live with his metaphysics. It involves us in falsities that destroy our equilibrium. It doesn't save us from the demonic quality of doubt and absurdity. Nothing redeems us from the demoniacal. We think of Descartes as the creator of "Method," as the thinker who experiences the *Cogito* throughout his life. This is the thinker who knew the demonic powers, those that dwelt in the human soul. No other philosopher was tortured with such doubts. No other philosopher dared to introduce us to these satanic powers. This is the Descartes we would prefer to forget, but this is the Descartes we should remember intensely. This was the great Descartes. The question of Descartes's relevance is irrelevant. We need to know, to experience, to feel the demonic doubts which tortured not only his soul, but ours as well.

* * * *

In a text called "Seconde vue de Descartes" (A Second View of Descartes) published in 1943, Valéry stated that Descartes's greatness may be summed up in two points: "He made a personal matter of what had before his time been treated in dogmatic form, dominated by tradition....He discovered that his Self tipped the balance. He felt strong in his own solitude, was able to answer for everything that he thought, observed, deduced, or defined *himself* as opposed to the quantity of doctrines, formulas, and purely verbal constructions kept alive only by the arguments of the schools and handed down from century to century." Valéry added a short but decisive remark, stating that Descartes "was first and foremost a will" ("A Second View of Descartes," in *Masters and Friends*, 69). I would move beyond the will to the torturing nature of the demons. These Valéry knew well. We are at that time in his writing when he carefully realized the satanic qualities that dwelled in him and marked the human experience. If there are ties that link Valéry to Descartes and Descartes to Valéry, then there is the realization of the demonic forces which are inseparable from knowledge. We no longer wonder at the Self that Descartes explored with confidence and fascination, but we turn also to the frightful magnificence of systematic doubt, of doubt in its known and unknown dimensions. We see in Descartes the true philosophical personality. Philosophical vocabulary reveals a struggling Self, an experience which every man finds within him, if one day, he decides to think. Descartes philosophizes for every man.

* * * *

We arrive at an imaginative essay that seduces us to approach but not to conquer, to read and not repeat, to walk away quietly and absorb personally the experience. It is a seashell to be seen and felt, to be conversed with, knowing that replies will not come, and yet they come. We will hear them in our peculiar listening. They will startle us and we will be content. They will become silent and we will be unhappy. We don't know how we will be unless we pretend that we are scholars seeking to classify and organize our material, but say little about it. The serious face will appear in all its fierceness. We hear the word *objective*, flying about in all directions, seeking to crush any species that would tempt us to follow another direction. We call upon the will to suppress the demonic. We yearn to be saved from the defining powers of man's created nature, from his need to be like God, from his desire to measure what was never measurable, to measure the *Je pense*. This *I* is man's precious breath. It is his belief in his unique creativity, in his power to break out of an artificial captivity, his realization that thinking is always the thinking of the *I think* exploring the objective and subjective nature of the subject. It does have two natures. The subject is always discovering itself as subject. He discovers the subjective and objective quality of the Self that says: *Cogito*.

Each essay of Valéry brings us to a new understanding of both author and subject. As we follow Valéry, we realize that we are following Descartes, and when it's Descartes we follow, we are aware that it is Valéry who has always been present, silent and veiled. We remove the veils slowly, uncovering other veils that have hindered our vision of truth.

The essay "Le Retour de Hollande" (1926) (The Return from Holland) is a series of images which reveal a simple fact: The life of a philosopher doesn't belong exclusively to the agenda he establishes. He becomes a living figure, not in what his disciples say is an orthodox reading of his text, but in the re-creation of his thinking by those who read him intelligently, those who bring with them a philosophical sensitivity, a philosophy of their own. "I am leaving Holland," Valéry remarked, "I suddenly have the feeling that Time is beginning; that Time has started to move; that the moving train has become the symbol of

Time with all its restlessness and its powers. It devours all visible things, shakes up all mental things, flings its massive body into a savage attack on the very face of the earth....It turns bridges into thunder, cows into projectiles, the pebbly surface of the roadbed into a curtain of machine-gun power" ("The Return from Holland," in *Masters and Friends,* 72). Suddenly we discover the forces of images. The imagination slips in as the intellect yields space. It embraces the intellect, speaks to it, and convinces it that its world is as powerful and meaningful as that of the intellect. It is the world of the metamorphosis, of the wonders of transfiguration. What is even more startling is the realization that the imaginative skills complement and strengthen their companion, give it a freedom it never before possessed. There are many methods, many ways of approach, many expressions and many vocabularies. I think of the expression "Time is beginning," and I wonder what is the significance of these three words. I must wait. I must read. I must think quietly, knowing only that my journey is not going forward but actually it is going backward. I am going backward in time, trying to relive the experiences which came to me when the *I think* brought me to the experience of the *Cogito.* Valéry asks us to take this journey with him and many of us do. We follow him not to learn how to repeat what he has said and done, but to learn what it means to have a philosophical experience. Some philosophers allow such an experience and some don't. This distinguishes the great from the insignificant.

Valéry mentioned that he had just been in Amsterdam. He noted that "Descartes was particularly fond of this town where, since there was not a single man except himself who was not engaged in commerce, he could remain all his life without ever being noticed by anyone and could walk around every day lost in the throngs of a great people" ("The Return from Holland," 76). Is it this solitude that creates the philosopher? Does he need to do something that the others don't do? It is doubtful. Any man may be called a philosopher who has chosen to think. Any man who has chosen not to think makes his life in business activities, in the military, in the church, in commerce, in academia. Descartes had always traveled, but his space never changed. Uninterrupted space makes it possible for him to entertain different views and attitudes. Each came forth like a passing light. He thought of it only for the moment. He saw it and it fled. Its reality belonged to a mind that would remember the train, the lights, the images and their changes. We are alone with thinking. In thinking, every man is in solitude. In this solitude, man realizes the misery and glory of the intellect. Thinking is the epitome of human progress. It is the nadir of the human effort. Descartes knew well how easily thinking is distorted, how it protects and advances the perverse. Descartes experienced the satanic, the demoniacal. We would advance the idea that it was the demoniacal that created the originality of Descartes's philosophy. Valéry, unhappily, did not bring us into the powers of the demoniacal. He kept an inexplicable distance. Descartes's philosophy was attuned to it and lived from it.

Every thinker belongs both to our imagination and to his own reality. Valéry noted that this was true of Descartes. "I count," he said, "on the fact that the thoughts of the living man were not quite the same as the ones he put into his books. Books always deceive us to some degree, more or less. What they fail to tell us about the writer and what they add, leaves plenty of room for anyone who wishes to imagine the author as he may have been." We may yearn for a power that would make it possible for us to reproduce what another has done, but we have machines for this. They do their work magnificently. How can I bring the other into my mind, and "imagine the author as he may have been"? ("The Return from Holland," 79). For this I have always thought that the demoniacal had a greater role in Descartes than we are willing to admit. For this reason, I believe that this satanic power is the lifegiver of human thought. Rather than being the negative power, it is positive, being the encounter in which we initiate the intensity of the human struggle in search of the *Cogito.* This we will hopefully never find. We find only formulations that make it communicable. There is always more. It is this more that intrigues us. The author, as well as the reader, discovers the book, each from his own perspective, each seeking to advance a distinct attitude. Each goes his own way.

We imagine Descartes in Amsterdam. He is the man in search of solitude, who struggles to find the unique philosophical experience, who is determined to do it because he must. Truth lies in him. He is sure of this. This truth was molded in the hands of The Deceiver. Descartes had left the doors open for the demoniacal. He knew that the *I think* was easily distorted and from it emerged a perversity that destroys both man and world. If God – not the One in the New Testament – will save us from The Deceiver, we long for his presence in us. We seek the truth that he embodies in his Being. We can't be sure that The Deceiver has not incarnated the idea in himself. Descartes has to believe it. There is no other choice. We can't imagine Descartes to be absurd.

Valéry sits on the train as it nears Paris. He describes the happenings: "The train slows down and comes to a stop on the outskirts of Paris. It picks up again slowly for the *finale....*A journey is rather like a symphony. The analogy extends even to the impatience of the people who stand up, put on their hats, get ready, and make for the corridors" ("The Return from Holland," 85). We know that we have traveled from Amsterdam to Paris. We thought of our thinking about Descartes, but we also thought about the ways and methods of our thinking. We find it unavoidable to set down a "Method," and at the same time to want to set it aside. We speak of how things are created in our consciousness, but we wonder about those things that escape it. Reality is greater than our idea of reality. It is greater than our existence. This is an existence that we command, and don't command. Valéry remarked that "while consciousness is rediscovering and giving names to things which are clearly defined, to the significant data of the picture, we are subjected at the same time to the subterranean and as it were, contingent action of the darker patches and areas of chiaroscuro" ("The Return from Holland," 82).

We think of these dark patches, these unknown and unexpected moments of darkness. An undefined unsurety returns, an uneasiness and fear cause us to doubt our enterprise, the values we have embraced, the truth we hope to arrive at. The political man knows that he can't share in the leisure of the philosophers, that their problems are not his. The statesman belongs to the realm of judgment, while the philosopher reflects on the nature of pure reason, finding categories and postulates to entomb existence. There are no bridges from one to the other. The statesman must, however, think. Thinking is no stranger to him. His aim is, however, decisions, positions, and attitudinal subtleties that avoid decisions. Valéry possessed a natural aptitude for subtlety. He was, among men, the wise gentleman; among the scholars, the poet; and among the philosophers he remained undefinable. They ignored him. What he offered them they didn't want to hear. They feared him. He enjoyed their fear. He enjoyed showing them their inadequacies. They experienced him in their living. They would not escape him. They could declare their ignorance of him. There is a happiness in this.

I end this chapter knowing that I have not ended it. I cannot end it. If I pretended such a foolish attempt, I would be filled with damnable doubts, and if they were not present, I would wonder about my sanity. But I don't want to wonder about my sanity. I want to assume it. I need to assume it. I assume it for the survival of the lie. Paradoxically, the lie is the source of sanity. I can live with it. I can live *well* with it. Without the lie I am left with purity, the most destructive aspect of man's nature. It brings with it a madness that affects other people. To know how well Euripides understood this requires only a reading of his play *Hippolytus*. We may be confused about our divine worship. We waver between the love of Artemis and that of Aphrodite. We are always wavering, maneuvering, and traveling. We are never sure. We fear surety. We turn to the lie and dwell there in comfort. The lie is the simple rejection of purity. Nothing else is, for the moment, opening its door to my mortality.

10

The Presence of Pascal

Shortly after his essay on Pascal appeared, Valéry wrote to his friend Pierre Féline: "The article on Pascal is everyday stuff; nothing worth communicating to any but the 40,000 readers of the Revue hebdomadaire" (see Pierre Féline, "Souvenirs sur Paul Valéry," *Mercure de France,* July 1, 1954, p. 417; note to "Variations on a Pensée," in *Masters and Friends,* 364). Valéry wrote his article to celebrate the third centenary of Pascal's birth in 1623. It is of little importance what a man thinks of his work. It is for others to judge, but only for the moment. There was something fascinating in the "pensée" that Valéry chose. It read: "The eternal Silence of these infinite spaces TERRIFIES me." Valéry suggested in his notes accompanying his text that "this eloquent phrase, the powerful impression it seeks to produce on our minds and the magnificence of its form have made one of the most famous sayings ever uttered, a Poem and not a Thought at all" (notes to "Variations on a Pensée," 86).

We leave aside for the moment this division between thinking and poetry. There is quicksand in the discussions about their distinct natures. I think of those two words, *poetry* and *thought.* I think of the terror of emptiness, the emptiness that reveals terror, that reduces our stature, that diminishes our thinking and causes a frightful diminution of both our intellectual and emotional powers. We have managed as well as organized Lilliputians. "The eternal silence terrifies me" is announced with gusto. It is a divine message that all human beings are capable of hearing and comprehending. This lack of comprehending doesn't bring fright. Men need not comprehend, nor need they hear too deeply. Images both comfort and frighten them. Vastness terrifies them. Silence crushes their equilibrium. This is what Pascal wants us to believe, to imagine, to think about. I wonder if it is anything more than the majesty of divinity, its presence, and the awareness of creation.

Valéry continued, in his notes, to write about the poetic quality of the "infinite" and "eternal." "Their impact," he said, "are symbols of non-thinking. Their impact is purely emotional. They have an effect only in a certain kind of sensibility. They arouse the particular feeling of being unable to imagine" (notes to "Variations on a Pensée," 86). We are awakened to a universe. This universe is not an abstraction. There is something sacred about it. We feel consumed by it. We have been reduced to the fleeting qualities of our feelings, but we no longer know how to think. We don't think about the eternal or the infinite. We accept them poetically. We envision them, dream of them, picture them in their negation. Suddenly, we realize that the heavens sing, that there are musical spheres which reveal a harmony that is nowhere else possible. "Just as the spheres are obedient to a law," Valéry noted, "so the sounds which they engender form the soft and gently varying harmony which is that of the heavens with the heavens. The world of pure order delights your ears" ("Variations on a Pensée," 87).

The singing heavens fill us with pleasure, even with joy. The sounds are as sublime as the silence. We find ourselves in a delightful paradox, moving in one direction to the sounds that attract our senses, and in another facing the immeasurable silence that shakes our being. The music brings us peace and tranquillity, the silence a melancholic fear that never leaves us. We fear its departure. It would leave us with a vague nothingness that we couldn't endure. The sweetness of the music would drive us into madness. We are not the children of the absolutes. They are the clarion calls of our death, the destruction of our humanity. We wonder if this silence speaks of death. We are sure that it does. We are sure, similarly, that the music deafens us to life.

Valéry reminded us that "there would be no poetry, it would never have been invented, if this peculiar accident had never occurred. There would be no poetry, were it not that industry and artifice enable the poet, by the practice of numerous substitutions, to multiply the number of lucky finds and to put together as many as necessary to compose a wholly pleasing continuity....So it is with children's sayings, sometimes so remarkable, whose grace and import are unperceived by their authors. Nothing of the kind in the case of Pascal" (notes to "Variations on a Pensée," 88). What is frightening in one universe is joyful in another. Whatever gives man contentment in the vision of the stars of heaven makes music for the divine dwelling. Under which heavenly canopy do we live? This has been a fundamental problem for man since he has begun to think. Augustine showed us two canopies; one he called the City of God, the other the Earthly City. From these we have lived. They allowed us to see both the joy of the stars and the weeping of the creative forces, man's most precious inheritance from his origins. "The stars sometimes appear to be confused with the sons of God who are the angels, and the countless tribes of spirits and stars resound over the whole earth in an immense acclamation" (notes to "Variations on a Pensée," 89).

How fascinating it is to wonder about the visions of the heavens! How dependent we are upon the judgments we make of the signs that the heavens give us! The joy with which we project ourselves to the heavens corresponds to the happiness that other beings find in themselves. The sadness of unhappy beings is lodged in the heavenly forms, while optimism of the many is painted in the heavenly dwellings. The man who takes pride in the creative powers of his being is conscious of his unique place in the universe. The one who is saddened by it has felt the disharmony that exists between divine and human life, between the powers of the human spirit and the pessimism which so quickly covers him when he expresses his failures and weaknesses. Man's success and disappointments belong to his yearnings, either to imitate the gods or to develop the fascinating forces that accompany the *I think*.

Valéry observed that for Pascal the infinite spaces have nothing to offer but silence. "He describes himself as 'terrified.' He complains bitterly of being alone in the world. He cannot discover Him in the heavens....'Terror,' 'terrified,' 'frightful,' 'eternal silence,' 'dumb universe' – such are the terms in which one of the greatest intellects that ever existed speaks of what surrounds him" (notes to "Variations on a Pensée," 91). We run to condemn Pascal. We reread the *Pensées* and ask ourselves how this man could have said these things to us. He has done much to us, much to the creation. He saw centuries beyond himself. He saw the beguiling conquests of the demoniacal. He saw it with a profounder despair than Valéry's beloved Poe. He saw it in such depth that we who follow him find it impossible to turn away from him, to add a few optimistic observations that he could never accept. Pascal had seen into the human heart with such extraordinary light that our words seem to be weak, distressed, and painfully incomplete.

We turn to events. We let them speak. We try to absorb them, but they are too much for us. Even the poets in their fabulous powers of description find us incapable of listening. I think for the moment of the Spanish poet Miguel Hernandez, of the Turkish poet Nazim Hikmet, the Russian poet Mandelstam, of prison memoirs revealing a world we could never endure. Terror has come to dwell in the innards of our world. It enjoys the publicity that our technology offers. I believe that it grows excited in it. I think of the poet Delmore Schwartz and his poem "The Heavy Bear Who Goes with Me," from *Selected Poems, 1938-1958*. It is this heavy bear that is with me, that is always at my side, who is "the hungry, brutish one in love with candy, anger, and sleep. He terrifies me.

He fills the earth and the heavens. He is the deceiver, the indifferent one, the one who never leaves our side, whose being is everywhere. No dwelling escapes his hunger, no change can do without his strength.

> Breathing at my side, that heavy animal,
> That heavy bear who sleeps with me,
> Howls in his sleep for a world of sugar
> A sweetness intimate as the water's clasp
> and modified by the new astronomy.
>
> (*Selected Poems, 1938-1958*)

"In a heaven swept by telescopes," Valéry said, "Pascal found, for his own part, a new reason to fear". He feared the conquest of the unconquerable, the terrors that lie in such a yearning for conquest. "He saw nothing in the world from which he couldn't extract his poison" (notes to "Variations on a Pensée," 90). He saw nothing from which the elixir of life would flow. Life belongs to neither the poison nor the elixir. It belongs to an indifference that seeks one and then the other, that needs to change one into the other. This transformation is never successful. We are terrified by what lies in the middle, that is neither fully the one nor the other, that consorts equally with the one and the other. We are frightened by man's consciousness, this man who realized the powers of the *Cogito,* who believed that in and through it man replaced the divine. The divine seems to have planned it this way. The history of man's development could end in no other consequence: the replacement of the gods. The gods had grown weary. Their mythologies were finished. Tired gods need more vigorous ones, those with poisons and elixirs. They need to excite men to struggle and to battle, to give life to thoughts.

Who is this intellect that is so close to the demoniacal, who finds existence so distressing, so filled with the poisons of The Deceiver? Pascal nobly commanded his language, knew how to face his enemies and debated with them, fully in command of his rhetoric. Valéry noted that "intellect suffers, describes itself, and bewails its lot like a hunted animal; and moreover, one that hunts itself and incites the great resources within it, the power of its logic, the admirable virtue of its language to corrupt everything in sight that is not distressing" (notes to "Variations on a Pensée," 91). The story doesn't end with these observations. They are what they are. Dwelling with them is an intellect which dives ever more deeply into the evil that veils existence, into the corrupting powers, and perhaps into the little lights that lie behind the veil, those which allow us to partially remove it and allow us to discover that the poison which fills creation is redeemable. Creation is not fixed. It is not a system built on divine laws. These man discovers. Even if Valéry could say that for Pascal "there is no created thing that does not remind it [the intellect] of its appalling state; some of them wound, others deceive it, all terrifying it so much so that contemplation never fails to make it howl for death" (notes to "Variations on a Pensée," 91).

The intellect bewails its imprisonment. It weeps for its impotence. It is hidden in Cassandra's soul, captured by Calypso, never knowing about its release. It knows that one day it will be released or it will die. The world is a greater dwelling than the little island land. Even in the prison of the demons, the intellect seeks to analyze and comprehend. Death is its final adversary. Pascal knew what the Teacher had already expressed: *Vanity* is the universal word for all that exists, that wants to exist, and can exist.

Valéry's criticism of Pascal seems to have been prepared to eliminate a thinker whose ideas penetrated his own to a degree that threatened them. Valéry had found a viable alternative to his own thinking. Pascal was not simply an opponent but a deadly adversary. We think of Luther or Calvin. We think of Descartes himself, and the collapse of medieval scholasticism. Pascal brought with him the instrument capable of destroying the human confidence in reason, of humbling reason. Faith, and faith alone, smashes through reason, handing it over to the faith of Abraham and Job. Of them Pascal remarked: "Solomon and Job have best known and best spoken of the misery of man; the former most fortunate, and the latter the most unfortunate of men; the former knowing the vanity of pleasures from experience, the latter the reality of evils" (*Pensées*, 174). Between Solomon and Job, a greyish world of possibilities emerges. It emerges from those antagonists who struggle for the human soul. One comes forth in the glorification and exaggeration of human knowledge. The other becomes deeply attached to the divinity who preserves the freedom to interfere in the world, change its course of development, and force it to wonder about the truth that lies within it.

Valéry remarked that the origin of Pascal's "undertaking to destroy human values in general is perhaps to be traced to some particular wound of his self-esteem. There are rivals so formidable that they can only be brought down by bringing down the whole of the human race with them" (notes to "Variations on a Pensée," 92). We are fascinated by this notion. Neither point of view will dominate permanently the other. There is no doubt that the balance will swing in one or the other direction, but rarely will it swing so sharply that it will eliminate the other. We face a perpetual movement giving preference to the one and then to the other. As long as there is life, perpetual movement will occur. We, however, cannot rule out the possibility that the equilibrium will be destroyed. Ideologies and parties will take again the place of parliaments, congresses, and legal systems. *Equilibrium* is a term that reveals our inadequacies and our madness.

Valéry follows Pascal. He attempts to find in him all the inadequacies which will strengthen his own position in the *Cogito*. We are fascinated watching Valéry at work, knowing that he has found an enemy that he wants to threaten and surpass. He sees in Pascal a serious rival to Descartes, serious because the separation of faith and reason is not only a logical way that faith ultimately, even if slowly, overwhelms and dictates to reason. Faith is an heteronomous attitude and activity, crushing limitations and every philosophical attempt to integrate it with philosophy. There God becomes an Idea, a First Principle, the Ground of Being. He becomes everything that he is not. This is how philosophy wants him to be. The believer rejects all the disguises, all pretense, and he cries out to the God of incomprehension, of miracle, of anger and compassion: What is your meaning to creation? This is the God he creates, the one he needs for his philosophical failures, the one he, at times, prays to in the poetic beauty of the Psalms. Pascal is a formidable opponent. His thought bears in it the revolutionary element that becomes dangerous to the thoughts around him. Pascal denies the efficacy of thinking. Pascal's denial is dangerous. He radically separates faith and reason, leaving each autonomous but disastrously powerful as they stand alone, face to face, proclaiming their virtues, telling us that they are the embodiment of truth and must be protected even if it requires the sacrifice of all forms of life. Fate hangs over a world abandoned by the divine. The world is given over to sin. The divine traces have paled and disappeared.

"I cannot help suspecting," Valéry stated, "that there is something systematic and labored about this attitude of perfect harmony, this absolute disgust. A well-tuned sentence is incompatible with total renunciation" (notes to "Variations on a Pensée," 93). It seems that we are entering a realm of explanations that are not convincing. Valéry draws a consequence that appears to be an exaggeration. We wonder if Pascal's attack on human existence is not the most efficient way to study it. His illustrations are often poetic, startling, and fascinating, filled with imagery and beauty of expression. Healthier than naive optimism is the blunt and shocking pessimism that allows us to face the world with a sense of maturity and prudence. Valéry raised two questions: "What do we teach other people by continually telling them that they are nothing, that life is in vain, nature hostile, knowledge an illusion? What is the point of belaboring their nothingness, or telling them over and over what they already know?" (notes to "Variations on a Pensée," 93). There is no point. The questions tickle our imagination. We take pride in knowing all that we should know. We turn to Pascal and we say: Why do you waste our time with things and descriptions that have been discussed through the ages, in fact, from the events in the garden of Eden or from Cain's murder of Abel? We are intelligent men and we have read Ecclesiastes, Proverbs, Greek tragedy, and the Minor Prophets. These are old texts and the circumstances in which they developed are usually unknown to us. Pascal is distant from us and we wonder if we understand him adequately. There is a decisiveness in him that terrifies us. We live our lives from the power of reason, and we believe deeply in them, in what we have accomplished and what we will yet accomplish with them. Reason doesn't function without faith. There is a faith in reason and we hold on to it dearly. We fear the weakening of this faith. We fear every attempt that falsely questions it, that brings doubt to it. Why should we be so devout in our belief? Perhaps we have no other beliefs. Perhaps we want to avoid any type of faith. We know the demons that follow it so ardently.

I wonder if Pascal's lack of enthusiasm for the created world was not the source of his greatness, his power to describe it with bitterness and disdain. Pascal sought a higher world, a deeper confrontation, one that not only terrifies us but drives us to challenge and confrontation. Negation has positive forces. Pascal suffered deeply but he taught us how to use the suffering for good purposes. In fact, it is in suffering that man is separated from his fellowman, that he learns that suffering is both companionship and disdain. We are brought closer to our fellowman in a suffering that reveals our common humanity. It is in reason that we discover the need to describe how we are affected by suffering. Should we be surprised when Pascal said, "Thought constitutes the greatness of man," or when he stated that "reason commands us far more imperiously than a master; for in disobeying the one we are unfortunate, and in disobeying the other we are fools"? (*Pensées*, 345). Pascal remarked that he could "well conceive a man without hands, feet, head. But I cannot conceive man without thought. He would be a stone or a brute" (*Pensées*, 339). The question that plagues us concerns the autonomy of reason. It doesn't concern reason, but its autonomy. It is a wager. We assume that reason is autonomous, drawing from itself the laws, i.e., the logic of its attitudes and movements. But it is possible to conjecture that reason is an endowment, a divine endowment that allows us to differentiate reason from its source, or forces us to identify the two. The injection of heart, as a fundamental aspect of the human act, complicates the problem. What does the word *heart* mean? A heart is a heart, but it is not. Now we can say whatever we want to say about it. We poetize it. We use it as a metaphor. We juggle the term and enjoy the game we are playing. We can also believe that the heart is the receptacle for the dwelling of the divine. In fact, we can do what pleases us. What do we owe to reason? In our doubts, we achieve its highest realization.

Valéry enunciated with delicacy and subtlety a rationalism that was not only logically, but morally and aesthetically, meaningful. He said that "as long as somebody still matters to us, our distress remains manageable; it may still be of use to us. And so our faith, if we have any, is therefore not so completely fixed on God that there is not some left over, some small faith in the judgment of people of taste, and some hope in the connoisseurs of fine literature. If I feel that all is vanity, the very thought prevents me from writing it down" (notes to "Variations on a Pensée," 94). Have we come to the conclusion that the realms of human thought are vaster than the embrace of the divine, that these realms are vaster, more encompassing, more directly involved in human life? We are sure that this life is only an aspect of thinking, that life and thinking are not one, that life can either be more than thought or thought more than life. How poor life would be if it were greater than thought! There is no reason to assume that God is greater than both thought and life. If the logical relationship confers superiority upon God, the experiential one gives superiority to thinking, to human existence. In a Pascalian universe, we are absorbed in God, feeling his presence in all that we do and think. We feel the vanity, the dread, the melancholy that accompanies our despair. This is the despair of the sinner, the one who feels the demoniacal that crushes his hopes and visions, his yearning to create, to be a contributor to the architecture of the future. With sharpness and decisiveness, Valéry struck at the heart of what he believed was Pascal's resentment. He said: "Can it or can it not be proved that Pascal only felt the joy of renunciation after first sufficiently corrupting, villifying, and poisoning the thing that he renounced? He would not vomit up the world if he had not already tainted it" (notes to "Variations on a Pensée," 96).

Why do thinkers need to taint the world and then to destroy it? We wonder if their own experiences were tainted. They seem to be surrounded in darkness. They have lost their place. They have lost their purpose. With amazing insight, Pascal remarked that "by space the universe encompasses and swallows me up like an atom; by thought I comprehend the world" (*Pensées*, 348). I wonder if Valéry would not say something similar. If any one of us didn't feel the embracing powers of space, didn't see ourselves overwhelmed and crushed by the space in which we dwelled by time that drew from us the strengths of body and soul, we would have surrendered our intellect, silenced the *Cogito*. There is liberation in thinking, that inordinate power which refuses to surrender to space or to time. Are they not in reality the same? They are the captors of human life. They struggle with thought. Thought is their enemy. It refuses to be held in a Calypso prison. It is always in exile. Thought knows no fixity, but thought has been fixed and repeated like a message. It easily becomes dogmatic. Thought dies quickly. It dies in the mouths of soothsayers, prophets, and the learned who are said to be close to divinity and have learned secret and sacred messages. Pascal has brought God too close to us. He has brought him to dwellings where his presence is destruction and distortion. Pascal described an intimacy that Valéry needed to reject. This intimacy perverted the nature of man. Pascal said that "all our dignity consists, then, in thought, by it we must elevate ourselves, and not by space and time which we cannot fill. Let us endeavor then, to think well; this is the principle of morality" (*Pensées*, 347). As we reread the *Pensées*, we have a distinct feeling that in every step of the divine approach to man, the act of destruction increases geometrically until the enormity of the divine presence is so great that man dies both emotionally and intellectually. Pascal shows us the realities of this death. He didn't tell us that a fervent prayer would ask God to send us from him.

Pascal observed that "man is but a reed, the most feeble thing in nature; but he is a thinking reed. The entire universe need not arm itself to crush him. A vapour, a drop of water suffices to kill him. But, if the universe were to crush him, man would still be more than that which killed him" (*Pensées*, 347). Closeness of God introduces a barbarized man. The autonomous realms which exist between the human and the divine are compromised. Both man and God face each other bluntly. This serves neither for man's sanity nor for his sense of equilibrium. The word of God burns and crushes what stands before it. The highest moment of God's love of man occurs when man, longing to approach the divine, is turned away. There is a world that needs his creative powers, a world that God must not touch. In a wishful remark, Pascal stated: "Man is neither angel nor brute, and the unfortunate thing is that he who would act the angel acts the brute" (*Pensées*, 358). The more I read Valéry's interpretations of Pascal, the more I am aware that in us there is a Pascal and a Valéry. Having one without the other is of little advantage and much foolishness. Either/or relationships excite our feelings for the extremes. They stimulate our disgust for what should be tolerated and comprehended. The extremes distort us. We become clowns and tightrope walkers. With this mad humor, man becomes the object of indifference. Whatever we say about him becomes doubtful, but whatever comes as a divine message we hold to be true. How do we hold a Pascal and a Valéry within us? How can we make them speak to each other? I see no way. We listen to two wisdoms. When we are attuned to one, we are deaf to the other. This is our despair. Pascal said: "To leave the mean is to abandon humanity. The greatness of the human soul consists in knowing how to preserve the mean. So far from greatness consisting in leaving it, it consists in not leaving it" (*Pensées*, 378).

I remarked previously that both a Valéry and a Pascal dwelt within us. We need them for balances to prevent that one-sidedness into which our intellect or feelings easily fall. I wonder if *balance* is the proper word. Balance has a way of deadening feelings. It places limits on the passions. Balance is often destructive to the creative energies which are the source of man's most distinct achievements. The intellect has its fascinating mobility of analyses, of syntheses, of confrontation with opposites, with the unexpected, the unknown, and the ambiguous. Balance seems to be the work of the weary, but is this true? Balance is an aesthetic achievement, the work of the architect, the artist. We turn from one direction to another. New visions appear to us. We see beyond our seeing. We hear beyond our hearing. Worlds appear superseding other worlds. The god Janus takes from us every vision we desire to preserve. Yes, there is a moment of balance in every great work, yes, every great work is an achievement belonging to the sense of organization and form. We speak here of method, but not of a fixed and imposed path or movement. We speak of "Method" as an explanation by which we are guided to the process by which the mind creates in its diversities. We comprehend; we do not judge Pascal. Comprehension leaves us sterile. It forces us to avoid the way of action. We listen to Valéry and we are hesitant in our attitude. We wonder if Valéry is conscious that he is dealing with an opponent he can't conquer and doesn't dominate. Pascal can't be conquered. He can be thrown aside. He would bubble up into a monster capable of dominating his opponents. We can ignore him, but this would be cowardly. It would be difficult to justify it to ourselves. A game has come into existence. It is one played by these two great minds. We watch because we know that we are an integral part of this game. We are Pascal. We are Valéry. We are both in diminished forms. We know this well.

Each of us yearns at one moment or the other to think like Valéry or to think like Pascal. Human events and human beings drive us to one extreme or the other. The panorama of world atrocities and self-mutilations affect us deeply, and there are the powers of human achievements, miraculous accomplishments. We visit them with wonder and a sense of greatness. We play the game of opposites constantly. The more perceptive and sensitive we are, the more perplexed the game becomes. What we have valued as good becomes in time dangerous. There are many ways to throw the ball into the loop. We care only for the activity itself. What is good and what is not is arbitrary. How often we have repeated with Pascal: "How I love to see this proud reason humiliated and suppliant!" (*Pensées*, 388). How often have we realized that this outcry is meaningless and purposeless! This is the pain that can't be cured. Only ignorance brings relief, only indifference blunts the edges of the pain. "Ecclesiastes," Pascal said, "shows that man without God is in total ignorance and inevitable misery" (*Pensées*, 389). We imagine how the statement could have been uttered. God is not the beginning of knowledge. The divinity can be lost sight of, when it is not mentioned and happily ignored. The presence of God draws confusion. It paralyzes reason and brings madness to human judgment. Pascal said: "My God! How foolish this talk is! Would God have made the world to damn it? Would He ask so much from persons so weak? etc. Skepticism is the cure for this evil, and will take down this vanity" (*Pensées*, 390). We would turn to Pascal and say quietly but seriously that all the answers belong to one word. They belong to that little word *yes*. We can think of anything and we can draw meaningful conclusions from it. Why should God not damn the world? The ways of God are not ours. What is asked of us is to explain the inexplicable. The experience of God brings only madness. We must run quickly from it. God exists for those who surrender their humanity, who have lost faith, the faith of reason.

Valéry, we can assume, knew the arguments that we could make for Pascal. He adds a thought that returns us to a contentful sobriety. He said: "But there is something lacking (a certain nobility) in all greatness which is not aware that it is accidental, and in every mind which fails to discern its own weakness and mediocrity as clearly and curiously as it recognizes in itself occasional beauties and insights which at times may be extraordinary" (notes to "Variations on a Pensée," 98). These reveal the strands that have been woven by Valéry to give his fellowmen a description of the wonders of human thinking. This is his clarion call. This is his courage and hope. We know that under the worst of conditions it will not die, nor can it surrender to absurdity. Yet there is always the hellish voice, this "imp of the perverse" that remains close to us and whispers constantly to us. It does not die. It does not surrender. We are terrified. We can't chase it away. It lives in the soul. It has always belonged to us. It is that devilish madness that smiles at our seriousness and confidence. We shudder at its presence. It is not victorious. It has never been defeated. We have no right to defeat it, but has it a right to conquer and dominate us? We are the children of a middle world. We belong to neither the positive nor the superlative. We belong to that exciting realm of the comparative, the realm of moral life.

Valéry was sure that we should avoid being apologists, something which today the "New Rhetoric" enjoins us to become. Its tools are persuasive and convicting of argumentation. To these people and to the tradition, Valéry remarked: "I cannot endure apologies. If there is one thing that a mind of great breadth ought to forbid itself, should not even conceive, it is the intention of convincing others, and the use of every means in its power to do so" (notes to "Variations on a Pensée," 98). Is not, however, the essence of conversation a degree of persuasion? Has not Valéry made the case for the Pascal approach to reality? "What is Eloquence? It borrows heat, images, metaphors, rhythms, to give vitality to statements which in themselves are nothing" (notes to "Variations on a Pensée," 100). Valéry is correct. Faced with God, we are tainted. If we are not, why are we taught to convince and persuade others to accept him? It seems to me that no teaching is without its rhetorical consequences. We are men in search of happiness, of something we call the peace of the mind. We fear its loss. We seek its continuation in God, in a divine promise, and above all, in a faith. We put the path of science alongside the path of faith, hoping that we can walk both paths with equanimity. We fail. The path of faith leads us indiscriminately to the unknown and arbitrary. The other takes us deeper into "Method" and organized experimentation. The one leaves us in the hands of interpreters, while the other leads us to a deeper and startling vision of the future of science. We stand at the threshold of a new scientific revolution that ties nation to nation, making us more and more conscious of the interdependence of human beings upon each other. Science has achieved what all the ideas of self-evident truths could never achieve. It achieved their self-realization. We still face the problem of the character of the scientist. What is the purpose of these developments, of these radical changes which affect so deeply our reason and feelings?

Valéry noted that "Pascal had 'found what he wanted,' but doubtless because he was no longer seeking. Giving up the search, and the manner of giving it up, may bring a sense of discovery. But he never believed in the kind of search whose object is unforeseen. He discovered in himself that *eternal silence* which neither genuinely religious nor genuinely profound men have ever observed in the universe" ("Variations on a Pensée," 107). Valéry complained vigorously against Pascal's eagerness to persuade. His persuasion was natural. Persuasion exists when the issue is doubtful and vague. Dictators learn how to persuade. They do it well. It is a professional activity. Persuasion appeals less to reason than it does to passion. It appeals to the heart, that vital organ that Pascal loved dearly. Valéry put it in his own terms. He said: "My complaint against Pascal is that he wanted to *persuade;* and for this purpose – as it always happens in such cases – he distorted, overstated, withheld, etc. As I see it, if a man has something to say and thinks it should be said, he should put it down just as it is in his mind – that is, with his objections, etc., always included. Exactly as it is" (*Notebooks,* 16:592).

Each philosophical perspective transcends sensibility. The very notion of philosophy is to express, in one way or another, the visions and comprehensions which men have had about mind, universe, and divinity. We find it impossible to pursue comparative analyses without a deadening fatigue, one that returns us to caves and leaves us dull-witted. If there is one thing that Valéry sought to convey to us, it was the belief in the richness of the imagination. We put thinker alongside of thinker, we compare thoughts with thoughts, and we declare that we are thinking and writing philosophy. In fact, we are doing nothing of the kind. We are writing histories or comparative studies. Philosophy is born in questions, in wonder, in the powers of transformation. Philosophy is born in the image of poetry. There it has lived and lives. It comes forth as philosophy when it reacts to the fact of the world, when it faces the forces of destruction and seeks to survive. The imagination is always on the verge of death, yet it does not die. No singular idea is large enough to embrace philosophy. The idea of the Self does. Philosophy lies in the *Cogito*; in the search for the *I think* it finds the powers of both thinking and imagining. Facing itself, the *I think* hovers over the yet-to-be discovered, the unknown. It lives from the confused idea, knowing that it is no less valuable than the clear idea. In each we seek the struggle of the mind to comprehend itself, to express itself, to imagine itself. The mind drives us beyond life, beyond the feelings, beyond perception. It forces us to seek our humanity in the intellect, in that unfathomable potentiality that *is* human life and its transcendence.

We pass through the labyrinth of human misery. We stand at the verge of a new scientific revolution. We are astounded, and we despair. We are convinced that human nature can be corrupted, that it absorbs easily the attractions of perversity. We are convinced that man is an infinite possibility of forms, of attitudes and nuances. He plays many roles in history. They are offered to him from many sources.

Valéry never leaves me. His subtlety and intelligence draw me ever closer to him. Whatever philosophy may come my way, I remain attached to my imaginary conversations with Valéry. Perhaps there is no other place for me to go. The conversations that have been developed over so many years have now become my fate. I believe that I control my words and thoughts. I have discovered that I am not the master of my fate. I am its child. The one mistake I can make is to forget this truth, but I cannot be sure that it is my truth.

Conclusion

I find conclusions difficult. The conclusion is nothing more than the opening words to a new beginning. At the end of his article on Pascal, "Variations on a Pensée," Valéry noted a thought expressed by Pascal in his "Mystery of Jesus." Valéry cited it: "Console thyself, thou wouldst not seek me if thou hadst not found me." I could similarly conclude with these words. I feel as if they express clearly and precisely my searches for a man who would speak to a civilization, cause it to think about itself, its past, and its future. I found this man in Paul Valéry, but I have only begun to find him. I believe that I will never find him. I will approach him from one direction or from another. He will elude me. It can't be otherwise. One truth alone is possible. I come closer to Valéry because he draws closer to me. He was, and will be, with me.

Speaking again of Pascal, Valéry remarked: "He discovered in himself that *eternal silence* which neither genuinely religious nor genuinely profound men have ever observed in the universe" ("Variations on a Pensée;" 107). Pascal may have had his silence. He had nothing else to offer to God. As he sought to draw nearer and nearer to him, the silence became deeper and more extensive. I despair at the thought of such silence. I feel for the moment only the conversation that filled Valéry's encounter with Descartes. I was for the moment a philosopher.

There is little doubt that the *Cogito* is the source of man's rational existence, of his search for the reality and experience of his thinking, of the undiscoverable *I* that thinks. I can conclude with the feeling that in the *Cogito* lies a mystery, one that can and cannot be spoken of. The mystery hides from the spoken word. It fills the space between the letters. It is a simple whiteness that can't be read, and yet we long to read it. I walk between a colorless, but deeply attractive, relationship. I am there, but unsure what it means to be there. I leave the reader with these few observations.

Appendix

An Afterthought That Has Become a Counterthought

"I discovered him at least thirty years ago – the Reverend Father Cyprian of the Nativity of the Virgin, a Discalced Carmelite, hitherto almost unknown. It was a small discovery no doubt, but similar to many a great one in having been, as they say, due to chance" ("Spiritual Canticles," in *The Art of Poetry,* 279). The find was in a large book. The title read: *The Spiritual Works of the Blessed Father John of the Cross...The Whole Translated into French by the Reverend Father Cyprian of the Nativity of the Virgin Discalced Carmelite* (1641) ("Spiritual Canticles," 279-80). Three hundred and fifty years passed, a magnificent poetic work lies unknown and with little chance of detection. The fates work oddly. Valéry comes across Father Cyprian and his translation. He doesn't merely read it, he is fascinated by it. A poem is not translated, it is reborn. It forms a new poem. The translator is a poet. He could not be otherwise. Father Cyprian was more than a poet. He was a gifted and highly sophisticated poet. He faced St. John of the Cross. This was an encounter of spiritual giants. It is clear that Valéry was attracted by the title. Undoubtedly, he would read the poems. His simple Spanish was enough. He saw through words.

Valéry gives us some warnings. For the serious reader, they are taken seriously. What are these warnings? The works "require a vital participation which is quite different from a simple understanding of its text. Understanding is, of course, necessary: it is very far from being enough " ("Spiritual Canticles," 280). We need not be told this, but we are sure that we are not always aware of what it means to go from poetry in one language to poetry in another. This can't be discovered through a law or some sort of revelation. It can possibly be found in the sympathy or empathy of the soul. We need metaphors and metamorphoses. We need signs and symbols. We need what doesn't emerge in consciousness.

We need the capacity to encounter the unknown power of hearing sounds and songs.

Valéry began his story in such a way that we realized how intense is the interplay of interpretation and empathy. I remember the works of the German philosopher Wilhelm Dilthey, texts which were given over to *Verstehen,* the understanding. Verstehen made it possible for us to become a part of the object under whose being we stood, but why be a part of the object? Valéry remarked: "The soul must absent itself from everything that suits its nature, that is, the sensible and the reasonable. It is only in this condition that it can be led to the highest contemplation. To dwell in the 'Dark Night' and sustain it within oneself, must therefore, consist in yielding nothing to ordinary knowledge – for all that the understanding can encompass, the imagination forge, and the will savor, is very unlike, and out of scale with God" ("Spiritual Canticles," 280). We wonder what we are searching for in the "Dark Night." We wonder if when approaching this darkness we had not surrendered the richness of the perceptive, the sensual world, the one that is truly an expression of God's creativity and, perhaps, of his love.

A thought enters our being, penetrates our hearing, and our sight, and finally becomes a part of our soul. The poet drives me forward, but I don't want to go in that direction. I don't want to go in any direction. I want the peace of nonmovement, of profound silence. Even our silence and immobility is a movement, a silence and that precious nonmovement. As we approach the divine, we feel certain that the law of gravity is changing, and yet we wonder if this is true. What we held to be valid in the works of Isaac Newton, or Albert Einstein, have changed, but not radically. Even the new direction that Einstein indicated has become newly interpreted, driving us in ever new directions. All we know is that we are on the road, that we have been granted a new direction. We are no more than directions. Saint John has shown us a way, but this way can never be declared absolute. This would be redundant. We are uncertain if we can walk upright, or need a ladder handed to us from the divine, or perhaps by a demon.

We think again of those words which Valéry cited: "Out of scale with God," and we wonder if there is anything that we do to make it possible to find a scale proper to God. Speaking of *The Ascent of Mount Carmel* and *The Dark Night of the Soul,* Valéry spoke of "the awareness of self and of a power of describing intangible things, of which literature – even that particularly devoted to psychology – offers few examples" ("Spiritual Canticles", 281). With caution, Valéry moves through a love poem that has now found its expression in his own language. Listen for a moment to the first stanzas of "Noche Oscura":

On a dark secret night,
Starving for love and deep in flame,
O happy lucky flight!
Unseen I slipped away,
My house at last was calm and safe.

* *

O night my guide!
O night more friendly than the dawn!
O tender night that tied
lover and the loved one,
loved one in the lover fused as one!

(*The Poems of Saint John of the Cross* , New Directions, 1972, 39)

It is not difficult for me to imagine Valéry's amazement and fascination at the beauty of these lines now so magnificently translated. The English text was prepared by the poet Willis Barnstone with the corresponding Spanish text. There is a beauty in Saint John that seems to sweep us toward the divine. Often I feel too close and want to retreat. The divine closeness suffocates me. I am deprived of the air which we humans depend upon, the air of distance. There is feeling in dynamic beauty that is unlike anything else I have found in an object or in nature. I fear this loss of breath, the friendliness of the night, the absence of all sensible attractions. I am not content with their disappearance, yet I wonder if I should trust my feelings. Perhaps they play games with me. I sound absurd, but absurdity is my condition, the one I assumed when I felt uncomfortable with God. I turn to Valéry and reread what he experienced.

Referring to *The Ascent of Mount Carmel* and *The Dark Night of the Soul,* Valéry said he was struck by the fact that both of these works are *"commentaries on poems...*I wondered what effects would be produced, in secular poetry, by this remarkable method which links to the poem its explanation by the author, even admitting that the author had something to say about his work, a fact that would be rarely counted against him." Valéry continued: "There is, in fact, nothing against thinking that the method adopted by Saint John of the Cross to communicate what one may call the harmonies of his mystical thought, while the thought itself is openly expressed close at hand..." ("Spiritual Canticles," 283). We have no doubt when speaking of the poetry of pure thought, a bit more doubt speaking of the poetry of speculative thought. Man's creative powers are forced into the poetical mold. From it they move toward a higher and more demanding communication. The problem is always communication. There the process of refinement begins and never ends, the word becomes precious and interchangeability is never arbitrary.

Communication lifts the soul, drives it toward deeper spiritual lights to that purity that reveals the uniqueness and wonders of thinking. However profound are the psychological and sociological explanations, they fail at the moment when the soul is touched by divinity, or what we call a transcendent power. I would imagine that it is this power which draws the soul from itself, revealing the mystery of a soul moving toward its beloved, knowing that this beloved is not outside the Self, but within it.

The grandeur of reason is immeasurable. It astounds us, forcing us to use such terms as *divine, godlike* and even *God.* We play havoc with our language when we indiscriminately manipulate the divine, juggling in its place, within and without our universe. Men have been so closely related to the gods that they created the one whom they believed created them. Their language becomes fuzzy. It flows in a fog, knowing nothing about clarity or limitation. We enjoy the language of mood, of sound, of movement, introducing thought to thought or melody to melody. In speaking of the genre of Saint John of the Cross, Valéry stated: "The model of the genre is undoubtedly the "Song of Songs" which...cannot dispense with an explication. Dare I admit here that all the beauties of that intensely rich poem leaves me somewhat sated with metaphor, and that the many gems that fill it end by antagonizing my Occidental soul and a certain abstract tendency of mind? I prefer the pure style of the work I am discussing. Enough of my own taste; it is of little importance" ("Spiritual Canticles," 284). It is of little importance, but at the same time it is of greatest importance. The lonely subject finds itself uttering opinions. It knows that it is speaking to the silence of the heavens. Slowly it turns upon itself and seeks to discover what it means to be a thinking *I*, what it means to be conscious of a thinking that is at the same time creating. Sadly we have limited reason to satisfy faith. The time has come to see faith in the expanded vastness of reason.

The problem is central to every religious experience. We use a vocabulary that is both adequate and inadequate, that brings us close and yet is distant from divinity. The problem remains our inability to know what it is that we call divinity, to formulate a way to come near to him. Our vocabulary frightens and mocks us. It may even terrify us. If we see reason in an expanding light, going beyond the analytical and synthetical, as containing within itself the attitude of faith, the reality of self-contradiction, of a hierarchical order of possible explication, then we have opened reason to potentialities it has never revealed but has harbored.

Valéry said that he saw the French text facing the Spanish. He read it. It was the text we had previously cited, opening with the words:

En una noche oscura
A l'ombre d'une obscure Nuict
On a dark secret night

The reader must go to the text. He must read, hear the words from within his soul, believe that the words have a dwelling within it. We begin to embrace the words as the words embrace us. This is the mutuality of love, the only love we feel, the only love that sings. "All at once, this text is no longer one intended to teach us something and to vanish as soon as that something is understood, its effect is to make us live a different life, breathe according to this second life, and it implies a state or a world in which the objects and beings found there, or rather their images, have other freedoms and other lies than those in the practical world....All this gives us the idea of an enchanted nature, subjected as by a spell to the whims, the magic, and the powers of language" ("Spiritual Canticles," 286). With modesty and charm, Valéry cited the stanza in the original Spanish. He spoke of his weak knowledge of the language, inducing the reader to approach the language and pronounce the words. The poem must sing.

With delight, we listen to Valéry's words about translation, a way of taking us from one world to another without imposing the one world upon the other. "He has not attempted," Valéry remarked, "to impose on French what French doesn't impose on or propose to the French ear. This is really to *translate,* which is to reconstruct as nearly as possible the *effects* of a certain *cause* – here, a text in Spanish – by means of *another cause,* a text in French" ("Spiritual Canticles," 286). In this creativity, man discovers the depths of the aesthetic. He finds a comprehension of beauty rarely revealed. He apprehends the relationship between beauty and movement, between the world of translation and the *Cogito,* a world bringing forth from itself another Self. Man is the carrier of a world to a world. He bears in his soul the bridges and the receptivities that make translations possible. We become aware that translations don't only belong to books of communication. They belong to every creative act. We are bringing ourselves from realm to realm, translating what we hear and see into what can be heard and seen. We are composing new possibilities, the yet unknown and the unexpected. In some way, we are translators in every realm of human activity. We call this freedom. The translator reveals the powers of thinking. He transforms realms of intelligence, leaving as undecided and unknown what others believed to have been decided and known.

Having read the first stanza of Saint John's poem, Valéry could say: "What followed overwhelmed me. I read with delight." Listen now to the second:

> Blackly free from light,
> disguised and down a secret way
> O happy lucky flight!
> In darkness I escaped,
> my house at last was calm and safe.

We listen again and we hear:

> A escuras, y segura
> por la secreta escala disfrazada,
> ¡Oh dichosa ventura!
> a escuras, y en celada,
> estando ya mi casa sosegada,

We listen again and we hear:

> En secret sous le manteau noir
> De la Nuict sans estre apperceuë,
> Ou que je peusse apercevoir
> Aucun des objets de la veuë...

We listen and we have listened. No, these are not three worlds arising from the mind, separate and fenced off from each other. These are three realms of human activity seeking the love which ties man to man, but each realm is unique. Each expresses in its distinct way the vehicle of this beauty and sound. We feel a sense of unity manifested in diversity. The languages are particular paths. We travel on one or the other. We go from one to another. No one path crushes the other. It only ignores it. We live in a world of comparisons. We reject the positive and we fear the superlative. Man begins at limits. He lives from his rejection of existence, caught up in the superlative. He denies transcendence. In the comparative, the god Janus reveals the need to go from one direction to another, to that comparative that has not eliminated either the positive or the superlative.

Valéry posed both a rhetorical and serious question about Father Cyprian: "Did ever a more flowing song – flowing but not slack – escape more happily from silence even in La Fontaine or Verlaine?" We draw near another stanza that enchanted Valéry:

> O my flowering breasts
> which I had saved for him alone,
> he slept and I caressed
> and fondled him with love,
> and cedars fanned the air above.
>
> (*Poems*, 39)

> Dans mon sein parsemé de fleurs,
> Qu'entier soigneuse je luy gardé,
> Il s'endort...
>
> ("Spiritual Canticles," 287)

We listen and lay aside the poem. It fades away in time. An aroma remains. This is all we have, but more would be heard if we could only listen to the sounds. I feel as if I am deluded. I receive only hints of beauty and tenderness. Why, I ask, have I been given so little? I don't even think of answers. I despair, knowing that I will never possess such a creative heat. I will remain the observer, the one who appreciates what he has not done. I can't penetrate this consciousness. I discover that I am wrong in my evaluation. I am only mortal, a being of limits, knowing only that I have no intuition of truth, that I fear in my inwardness any approach to divinity. I pray to be sent away. I pray for God's mercy, asking him to return me to my mortality. I often wonder how the poet creates the intensity that finally overwhelms us. Words force us back to it again and again. There is a constant rereading, a never-ending speculation and emotional pleasure. "A work," Valéry wisely said, "should inspire the wish to reread it, to recite its lines over and over, to carry them within myself for perpetuality. In persistent reading and repetitions, however, the attractions of contrast and intensity vanish: novelty, strangeness, and shock exhaust their quite relative effect, and what remains, if anything remains, is only what withstands repetition" ("Spiritual Canticles," 288-89). We despair. We hope. We seek the mystery of creativity. Why should we receive it?

It becomes clear what is Valéry's concern with perfection. If we often find the word difficult to comprehend but nevertheless use it arbitrarily, we are sure that our use is not arbitrary and obscure. If the word doesn't designate a particular form, a unique articulation, a clarity of expression, then it is a term that loses its significance and hides in words like the ongoing search for beauty. "What we call *perfection*," Valéry remarked, "eliminates the person of the author, and therefore does not fail to arouse a certain hint of mysticism – as does every quest whose bounds are deliberately set at infinity" ("Spiritual Canticles," 289). In listening to these poems, hearing them in three languages, it makes us aware that it is of little importance to know much about Father Cyprian. What would we know? How would this knowledge increase our capacity to listen to Saint John? I am sure that the melodies, the architecture, and enchantment of reason would not increase if we knew much about Father Cyprian. We know little about him. He was a great poet. We love Saint John, we read him in French. The languages poetize his love poems. How wonderful a gift is this poem given by a little known Carmelite. We are often perplexed by the relationship of autobiography and thinking. In Descartes we found it essential, it was the vital element of his thought. With Father Cyprian, it is quite unessential. Why don't we want to find a fixed attitude determining for us the proper way to understand a poet, or a philosopher? No understanding is perfectly fixed. No understanding is applicable to every human situation. In fact, it is the understanding which prevents such a transfiguration. The understanding is by its nature an openness to multiple possibilities, never captured by a divine or universal law. When the understanding speaks of perfection, it refers to a vast frontier of forms seeking to metamorphosize realities that live in time and space. In this search for transformation, thinking finds the purpose of its reality.

We try to bring the thought and poetry into a companionship, but we can't. Thought has its objections and poetry demands sound and expression. Thought must be justified in definition and elucidation. If we read the first section of Kant's *Critique of Pure Reason,* we know immediately that we are far from poetry. Thought dominates its object and we obey this domination with a style that must be adequate to it. Each human activity demands a style. The style is not present. It needs to be discovered. Valéry noted that "all thought that has to define and justify itself to the extreme limit dissociates and frees itself from rhythm, number, and resonance – in a word, from all pursuit of the sensuous qualities of speech. A proof does not sing" ("Spiritual Canticles," 292).

We listen again. We have learned to listen. We know that the thinker and the listener belong to each other. What comes from them may be different, but they need each other. The thinker must listen to what the poet says and the poet must know the thinker's method but not imitate him. Listen to these lines of Saint John that Valéry cites:

> How lovingly and soft
> you make my breasts recall
> where you lie secretly
>
> *(Poems,* 56)

> !Cuán manso y amoroso
> recuerdas en me seno,
> donde secretamente sólo moras

> Combien suave et plein d'amour
> Dedans mon seins tu te réveilles
> Où est en secret ton séjour
>
> ("Spiritual Canticles," 292)

Poetry affects us immediately. It comes to us as a gift. We know that it is a gift. We cultivate it. Thought may come more naturally to us. Its language is more suitable to our habits. We long for a language that sings, that allows the beautiful to emerge. We declare it to be the beautiful. I quote Valéry's words because I have made them my own. I now live with them. These are the words: "For me poetry should be the Paradise of Language, in which the different virtues of this *transcendent* faculty, united in their use, but as foreign to each other as the tangible is to the intelligible, and as the immediate force of sound is to the development of thought, can and must come together to form in time an alliance as intimate as body and soul" ("Spiritual Canticles," 294).

Thought and poetry have vast horizons to approach. We approach the universes of humankind. We feel within ourselves the awakening of forces that will change our existence and metamorphosize our reality. Poetry, as well as thought, needs to envision the future. They both must speak to men and women everywhere. Poetry is a rare and distinct universality. Thought is universal in its search for truth. They will never dissolve into each other. Perhaps they can walk alongside each other?

We walk uneasily toward the unknown. It plagues our consciousness, and wearies our energies. We believe in reason in its yet-to-be discovered potentiality. I believe in the fantastic and its fascinating speculations. In the midst of our melancholic indifference there is hope, small lights of joy. We struggle to keep them alive. We cultivate them. We need the sparkling of the lights. Valéry took us into the poetry of beauty. We follow him. He has now left us. We travel alone. There is no other way to travel.